Praise for

An Invisible Thread
A Young Readers' Edition

"The lifelong lessons you learn challenge you to be a better you.
I think it should be required reading for middle schoolers; we could all
learn a lesson from Laura and Maurice's relationship."
—**Clare Goldsholl, thirteen years old, seventh grade**

"[*An Invisible Thread*] shows you can overcome difficult obstacles."
—**Grace Goldsholl, nine years old, fourth grade**

"I felt happy, nervous, and excited for Maurice at times while reading it.
This book taught me about kindness, thoughtfulness, and selflessness."
—**Juliet Jackson, ten years old, fifth grade**

"I particularly liked how Maurice was so confident and positive. It made me
realize how lucky me and my friends are and how easy our life is."
—**Dashiell Lubsen, nine years old, third grade**

"I felt like Maurice and Laura were there with me sharing their story
and special friendship. I learned that even when things seem hopeless,
there are people who really care and will help."
—**Ella Michalisin, ten years old, fifth grade**

"We should all help each other more.
I think Maurice and Laura are great role models."
—**Liam Michalisin, thirteen years old, seventh grade**

"In Laura's situation, she was able to help change Maurice's life
by being kind, and this is amazing."
—**Calli Reid, eleven years old, sixth grade**

"[*An Invisible Thread*] taught me to treat people with respect
and with kindness. After reading this book I will now be more
grateful for the things I have and the family I love."
—**Lila Smith, eight and a half years old, third grade**

an invisible thread

Also by Laura Schroff and Alex Tresniowski

An Invisible Thread Christmas Story

an invisible thread

A YOUNG READERS' EDITION

Laura Schroff &
Alex Tresniowski

Simon & Schuster Books for Young Readers
New York • London • Toronto • Sydney • New Delhi

SIMON & SCHUSTER BOOKS FOR YOUNG READERS
An imprint of Simon & Schuster Children's Publishing Division
1230 Avenue of the Americas, New York, New York 10020
Text copyright © 2011 by Laura Schroff and Alex Tresniowski
This young reader edition is adapted from *An Invisible Thread* by Laura Schroff and
Alex Tresniowski published in 2011 by Howard Books
Jacket photographs copyright © 2019 by iStock
All rights reserved, including the right of reproduction in whole or in part in any form.
SIMON & SCHUSTER BOOKS FOR YOUNG READERS
is a trademark of Simon & Schuster, Inc.
For information about special discounts for bulk purchases, please contact Simon &
Schuster Special Sales at 1-866-506-1949 or business@simonandschuster.com.
The Simon & Schuster Speakers Bureau can bring authors to your live event. For
more information or to book an event, contact the Simon & Schuster Speakers
Bureau at 1-866-248-3049 or visit our website at www.simonspeakers.com.
Jacket design by Greg Stadnyk
Interior design by Hilary Zarycky
The text for this book was set in ITC Berkeley Oldstyle Std.
Manufactured in the United States of America
0419 FFG
First Edition
2 4 6 8 10 9 7 5 3 1
CIP data for this book is available from the Library of Congress.
ISBN 9781534437272 (hardcover : alk. paper) | ISBN 9781534437296 (eBook)

To all the children like Maurice—never lose hope
and never stop dreaming, because the power of dreams can lift you.

And to all children who will never be food-deprived—
always count your blessings and keep sharing threads of kindness.

—LAURA SCHROFF

NOTE TO READERS

This book is based on the true story of Laura Schroff and Maurice Mazyck. Some events have been condensed, rearranged, or slightly dramatized to better suit young readers.

an invisible thread

MAURICE WOKE UP IN the closet.

This was where he woke up most mornings. A small, dark closet. He slept there because it was the only quiet place in the apartment where he lived. The apartment was only one room, and sometimes as many as eleven people lived and slept there at the same time. The room had only two single beds, where his two older sisters slept, and his aunt, and maybe a cousin or two. The beds had no pillows, no blankets. Over in one corner there was a chair and on the opposite side was a half a fridge and a small TV. And that was it.

There were always at least four or five grown-ups around, staying up late and making lots of noise. That's why, some nights, Maurice sneaked away to the closet, closed the door behind him, curled up, and drifted to sleep on a thin mat on the floor. It was a little cramped, and kind of spooky, but at least it was his own private space.

Maurice was eleven years old. He was tall for his age, but

skinnier than most of the other eleven-year-olds he knew. His burgundy sweatpants, which were a few sizes too big, barely stayed up on his waist. He had no choice but to wear them, even when they were dirty, which they always were, because they were the only pants he owned.

On this September morning Maurice woke and eased open the closet door. He stretched his long arms up toward the sky and looked around the apartment. Since there were no curtains on the windows, the room was filled with sunlight. Even so, everyone in the room was still asleep. Maurice counted the people—one, two, three . . . ten. Ten people, not including him. His mother, Darcella, was sleeping. Maurice went over and nudged her shoulder to see if she would budge, but he had no luck. His mother had a funny look on her face that Maurice was very used to seeing. The look meant she was off by herself in some far-off world, and she couldn't be reached.

Maurice's mother was sick. He understood that. He wasn't sure what her sickness was, or why it made her act the way she did. He just knew that Darcella couldn't always be like other moms. She couldn't always buy him new clothes, for instance, or make sure he had a warm bed to sleep in. She couldn't always remember if he was fed every day. Stuff like that.

But just because she was sick didn't mean she didn't love him. Maurice knew his mother loved him more than anything in the world. She just couldn't always show it, because of her sickness.

Over in the corner, in the only chair in the room, sat

2

Maurice's grandmother, Rose, her eyes closed. Maurice couldn't tell if she was asleep or just resting. Either way, he didn't want to go near her. Grandma Rose was a tough lady. She was a tiny little thing, just shy of five feet, but she wasn't afraid of anything or anybody. Grandma Rose spoke her mind and said whatever she was thinking, even if it upset everyone around her. And if someone got sassy with her, she might even take a swing at them. Knock them right in the nose. People in their community knew Grandma Rose didn't take well to being disrespected. The way to deal with Grandma Rose was to just let her be.

Yet when it came to Maurice, Grandma Rose was sweet and kind. She had a real soft spot for her grandson. "You're a good child," she told him all the time. Grandma Rose looked out for Maurice and made sure he knew she'd always be there to protect him. For Maurice, Grandma Rose's attention was like a great big beautiful gift, and he loved her just like he loved his mother. For a brief moment he thought about going to her chair and nudging her to see if she was awake, just to have someone to talk to, but he decided against it. Better to just let her be.

Maurice looked around the apartment. His two sisters, Celeste and LaToya, were asleep on one bed as usual, twisted around each other, arms and legs everywhere. Maurice's aunt and her two young children, Maurice's cousins, were asleep on the other single bed. Three grown men were asleep on the floor. Maurice recognized them—they were his uncles. Uncle Juice, Uncle Big, and Uncle Old. Maurice's uncles came and went

3

from the apartment, and Maurice never knew if they would be there or not. Sometimes they stuck around for a few weeks; other times they just dropped in for a little while. Maurice had three other uncles, and sometimes they slept there too. They were all nice to him most of the time, but they all seemed too busy to be bothered with him much. Mostly they ignored him.

Maurice understood that the adults in his life didn't have much time for children. That's just the way it was. As far as Maurice knew, it was the same for kids everywhere. So why would his life be any different?

Maurice went over to the small, half-size refrigerator that was sitting on the floor of the apartment. A tiny television sat on top of it. Maurice opened the fridge and looked inside. The lightbulb was missing, but he could still make out the layer of grime coating the single shelf. And he could tell there was no food. No milk or butter or cheese slices or anything. Just a bottle of water and a box of baking soda, which Maurice knew not to touch. Another side effect of his mother's sickness—she couldn't always remember to stock the fridge.

Maurice felt a familiar pang in his stomach. It felt like he'd swallowed a heavy rock and now it was just sitting there inside his belly, weighing him down, making him miserable. It was a dull, endless ache. Like someone had punched him in the gut.

Hunger.

Maurice hadn't eaten anything in two days. Two *whole* days. His body was crying out for food.

Okay, okay, Maurice thought. *Time to find something to eat.*

Maurice pulled on his dirty burgundy sweatpants and threw his matching burgundy sweatshirt over his head. Then he slipped his feet into his scuffed-up white sneakers that were one size too small and had ripped shoelaces. He didn't go into the bathroom to brush his teeth, because he didn't have a toothbrush. He remembered having one a long time ago, but it disappeared. And, anyway, the bathroom wasn't even in the apartment. It was down the hall. They shared it with everyone on the floor, and it was almost always occupied.

Maurice didn't have a lot of things. For instance, he didn't have a Game Boy, or a football to toss around, or a little race car to wind up and race across the floor, or a bicycle. He didn't have new sneakers or a winter coat or a hat or gloves or scarf. Come to think of it, he didn't have a home, either. Not really, anyway—the apartment where his family was staying was only temporary. Every place he'd ever lived was temporary. Soon, Maurice figured, they would get kicked out and have to find another place to live. *Homeless* is what people called it.

Most kids spend their whole childhood in the same home. In his eleven years, Maurice had already lived in *twenty different places*.

That's what it meant to be homeless. It meant never getting to feel like you were safe in one place.

Birthday parties. Maurice didn't have those, either. He couldn't remember ever having one. Sometimes he wasn't even

5

sure how old he was. Was he eleven or twelve? Maybe someone forgot a year in between?

Maurice had never taken a family vacation. In fact, he had never been outside of New York City. He'd never even stepped on grass. He didn't know what it was like to play on a swing set, or drink a glass of fresh-squeezed orange juice. These things just weren't a part of his world.

In Maurice's world, the only thing that mattered was being able to take care of himself.

Luckily for Maurice, he was a tough little guy. As tough as Grandma Rose. Well, maybe not that tough, but pretty tough for a kid. And even though he didn't have a father—his dad left when Maurice was just six years old—he had a mother who loved him, a grandmother who was kind to him, two sisters who could make him laugh, and several uncles who liked him well enough. Maurice had a *family*. Maurice believed that if you have your family, you are doing pretty good.

Maurice didn't feel unlucky. Sure, some kids had it easier than him—he knew that from looking through department store windows and seeing kids his age getting new clothes or new toys, especially around Christmastime. He could tell from the way some people dressed, in fancy suits with fancy shoes, that they had lots of money, while his family didn't. But not once did Maurice ever feel sorry for himself, because as far as he was concerned, he was doing just fine. What good would feeling sorry do, anyway? Better to mind his own business and keep taking care of himself. Which today meant finding food.

Maurice knew what had to happen. Whenever he was really starving, he would go out and stand on a street corner and ask strangers passing by for money. A quarter, a nickel, a penny—and on a very lucky day, maybe even a dollar bill. Whatever they were willing to give.

If enough people gave him a few coins, he'd be able to go to the pizza parlor on Broadway and buy a single slice of pizza—delicious, cheesy pizza, his favorite.

And if he got really lucky, maybe he'd even get to buy a cheeseburger and French fries at McDonald's, on Fifty-Sixth Street and Eighth Avenue, his favorite place of all.

And if he got really, *really* lucky, maybe he'd have enough coins left over to go to the arcade on Broadway and play a video game like Asteroids, which cost a quarter. It was one of his favorite things to do and he was actually pretty good at it, even though he didn't get to play arcade games too often.

Maurice went over to his mother and kissed her lightly on the cheek. Then he slipped quietly out the front door. The long hallway was dark and dirty. No one ever came around to vacuum the floors or wipe out the cobwebs. The lights were busted and the carpet had long since been ripped out. The walls were stained and covered with graffiti, and the hallway smelled of grease and mold. Maurice ran quickly past all the old newspapers and empty bottles on the floor, and flew down five sets of stairs, three steps at a time, to the lobby. Then, with one final burst, he was out of the building and on the street.

In a way, the streets of New York City were Maurice's real

home. He knew the streets. He understood the streets. He *owned* the streets. On the concrete sidewalks, no one paid him any attention, which meant he could do whatever he pleased and go wherever he wanted and no one would say a word about it. No one cared. No one worried. It was like he was invisible.

Maybe that was his superpower—invisibility.

Maurice liked it that way. But sometimes a man or woman would give him a dirty look if he got too close to them, or they would take big steps to move away from him. A mother with a baby stroller might speed up to get past him more quickly, as if just being near him was a problem. Maybe they thought he would take something from them, which was ridiculous, he'd never taken a single thing from a stranger. But, mostly, everyone left him alone.

Maurice turned the corner of Fifty-Fourth Street and marched up Broadway, the biggest and longest avenue in Manhattan. It was the busiest, too. People were always on their way in and out of delis and diners and office buildings. Lots of people. So many that they formed a kind of rolling human wave that swept down the sidewalks of Broadway, brushing past him and nearly swallowing him up. Maurice had to dart left and right to dodge all the adults streaming past him to their destinations. Finally, he arrived at the corner of Fifty-Sixth Street and Broadway—his favorite corner. He stood on a square of the sidewalk—his spot—and he stuck out his right hand and said what he'd said probably a million times before.

"Excuse me, can you spare any change? I'm hungry."

The human wave rolled past him. People in fancy suits and fancy shoes. They didn't stop or look at him or ask him why he was there—they just kept moving. They had their own lives, their own problems. Or maybe he was just too little, and they didn't even see him. Maybe Maurice actually *was* invisible.

Then a pretty woman, nicely dressed, with brown hair down to her shoulders, caught his eye. She was about his mother's age, and she had a kind face. Maurice had learned to read people's faces, and sometimes he could tell when someone would stop and give him some change just by their expression. This woman was walking fairly fast, like everyone did in New York City, always in a hurry to get where they were going. But something about her felt different. Maybe she would notice him. Maybe she would stop. Maybe she would be the one. Maurice had a good feeling as she got to where he was standing.

When she was right in front of him, Maurice stuck out his hand and put on his best smile.

"Excuse me, lady, do you have any spare change?" he said. "I'm hungry."

For a split second the woman looked down at Maurice. They made eye contact. She had heard him, and now she had seen him. He wasn't invisible anymore.

And then . . .

"No," the woman said as she looked straight ahead and kept on walking.

Maurice watched her walk away. He watched her start to cross Broadway, to the other side of the avenue. *Oh well*, he thought. *Just keep asking, someone will stop. Forget about her.*

And just when he thought that, something strange happened.

Out of the corner of his eye, Maurice saw a woman standing in the middle of Broadway—right in the center of the street, with cars and trucks and taxicabs coming straight at her!

And it wasn't just any woman—it was the same woman who had walked right by him! The woman with the kind face. Maurice watched as she stood there, looking confused, until a taxi driver blasted his horn.

"Hey, are you crazy, lady? Get out of the street!" the driver yelled.

The sound of the car horn startled the woman, and suddenly she turned around and began walking. But now she was walking back to the side of the street where she had started moments ago.

She was walking straight back to Maurice.

2

THE WOMAN CAME UP to Maurice and stopped right in front of him. He quickly shot out his hand again and asked, "Can you spare any change? I'm hungry."

And what happened next had never happened to Maurice before, ever.

"If you're hungry," the woman said, "I'll take you to McDonald's and buy you lunch."

Her answer startled him. She would buy him lunch? A whole lunch? And at McDonald's!? That was almost too good to be true.

Maybe it *was* too good to be true, Maurice wondered. Was this woman messing with him? What did she have in mind? No one had ever offered to buy him a whole lunch before. No one had ever offered to give him anything more than a dime or a nickel they happened to have in their pocket. This had to be some kind of joke. But—what if it wasn't?

"Can I have a cheeseburger?" Maurice heard himself ask.

"Yes," the woman replied.

"How about a Big Mac?"

"That's okay too."

"How about a Diet Coke?"

"Sure."

"How about a chocolate milk shake and French fries?"

Just talking about all that food made Maurice's stomach hurt even more.

"You can have anything you want," the woman said. "There's just one thing."

"What?" Maurice asked.

"Is it okay if I join you?"

The woman wanted to have lunch with him? What was *that* about? She didn't even know him. Couldn't she just give him some change and go away? Why would she want to actually sit down and have lunch with a stranger? Maybe she was one of those women who came around from Child Protective Services, the city agency that looked after kids in bad situations. Maybe she wanted to take him away from his mother, from his family. Could he trust her? Should he just run away?

After all, he knew the number one rule on the streets. It was a simple and straightforward rule, and it was the one thing you could never, ever forget.

No one does nothing for nothing. Don't trust no one.

Even so, all those questions and concerns and even the number one rule were all being overruled by the deep grumbling sound in Maurice's belly—an urgent plea, *Get food now!*

"Okay," Maurice finally said.

"Okay, then," the woman replied.

The McDonald's was right around the corner, on Fifty-Sixth Street and Eighth Avenue. Maurice and the woman walked up the block together, though he walked a little behind her, in case he needed to run. Maurice was always ready to bolt. Neither of them said a word as they walked. Maurice was relieved. He didn't feel like answering any questions. After all, they were strangers. Complete strangers. She was a grown-up, he was a kid. She dressed nice, he didn't. She lived in one world, he lived in another. What did they have in common? Nothing.

"I'm Laura," the woman finally said.

"I'm Maurice."

"Nice to meet you, Maurice."

They walked into McDonald's, and the strong smell of fresh French fries made Maurice's heart beat faster. They stood in the line to order, and when it was their turn, Maurice asked for a Big Mac, large fries, and chocolate milk shake. He was so hungry, his legs were shaking. Laura ordered the same thing. She paid for their food and they sat down at a table by the window. Maurice ate his Big Mac so fast, it was probably gone in about twenty seconds flat.

It might have been the best thing he'd ever tasted in his life.

Maurice didn't look at Laura while he ate. But he knew she was watching him. He could sense it. She was probably shocked at how fast he was eating. Maybe she'd never seen a kid so hungry before. Maybe she was wondering when he'd eaten last. Or maybe she was trying to figure out what he was doing on a street corner asking strangers for money. In New York City, there were plenty of people on the streets begging for change. But nearly all of them were grown-ups. Maurice had never seen another kid like him on the street asking for change, and probably neither had Laura. She was probably feeling sorry for him. Oh well. At least he was getting to eat.

Maurice had already sized Laura up, because that's what he did with all new people. He got a read on them. He paid attention to what they were wearing and how they moved and the way they talked so he could figure out if they were a threat. With Laura, his instincts told him she wasn't a threat. She wore nice pants and a nice shirt, so she probably worked in an office somewhere. But she didn't act like someone who worked for Child Protective Services. The people who worked there were hard faced, and they always looked tired and mad. Laura didn't. Her face was open. She smiled a lot. Maurice guessed she wasn't one of the superrich New Yorkers he sometimes came across. Those people *never* stopped and never even glanced at him. She was somewhere in between. Not superrich, but she definitely had more money than Maurice.

Which didn't say much, because Maurice had no money at all.

One thing was for sure, though—Laura was one of *them*.

Maurice divided New York City into two groups—*us* and *them*. *Us* were the people like him. These were the people who for different reasons didn't have a job, or were sick, or were poor; the ones who needed a helping hand. There were a lot of poor people in New York City.

Them was everyone else.

And now here he was, sitting at a table in McDonald's, across from one of *them.*

For a while Maurice and Laura ate their food and didn't say a word. The only sound was the loud gurgling noise Maurice made when he sucked the last of his chocolate milk shake through the straw. When Maurice finished—which was in less than two minutes—he fidgeted a little in his seat. Suddenly, he felt uncomfortable. What now? Should he just get up and leave? He got what he wanted, what he needed, so what was he supposed to do?

But no, he thought, *that wouldn't be right.* She had been nice to him. The least he could do was be a little nice to her in return.

"Where do you live?" he finally asked her.

Laura looked out the window and pointed at a high-rise building across the street. It was called the Symphony, and it had to be forty stories tall. Maurice had walked past it many times, and he'd always noticed how fancy the lobby was. Everything was bright and shiny. A man in a proper uniform stood outside the revolving door to make sure no one who didn't belong there wandered in.

"I live right there," Laura told Maurice.

"You live there?" Maurice asked.

"Yes."

"You live in a hotel too?"

"Well, it's not a hotel," Laura said. "It's an apartment building. I rent an apartment there."

"Oh," said Maurice. "Like the Jeffersons?"

The Jeffersons was a TV show that Maurice loved to watch whenever he had the chance. It was about an African American couple who moved into a large apartment in a luxury highrise building in Manhattan. The Jeffersons were the only African American people Maurice knew who lived in such a fancy apartment, and they weren't even real.

"Well, yes, like the Jeffersons," Laura said, "but my apartment is not as big as theirs. It's a studio. Where do you live, Maurice?"

He hesitated. For a few moments he looked down and didn't say anything.

"I live in the Bryant Hotel on Fifty-Fourth Street," he finally said.

The Bryant Hotel wasn't anything like the Symphony. Many years ago it had been a fancy hotel. But then it was taken over by New York City officials, who used it to provide housing for families that couldn't afford their own apartments. It had a reputation for being a dangerous place to live. It was run-down and dirty looking, and no one was in charge of fixing it up or making it safer. If you lived there, you were one of the forgotten people. It wasn't a place anyone would want to go in, yet that was where he lived.

The amazing thing, Maurice realized, was that he and Laura lived only two blocks apart. He was on Fifty-Fourth Street and she was on Fifty-Sixth Street. Just two city blocks separated them.

But they might as well have lived on different planets.

"I work at *USA Today*," Laura said.

Maurice didn't say anything, because he didn't know what *USA Today* meant.

"It's a newspaper," Laura continued. "It's the first national newspaper in the country. My job is to sell advertising space. That's how the newspaper pays for itself. By getting companies to pay us to advertise in it."

"What do you do all day?" Maurice asked.

Laura told him about her typical schedule—making sales calls, going to meetings, giving presentations, having lunches and dinners with clients. None of it made much sense to Maurice, but it sounded like a lot of work.

"You do that every day?" he asked.

"Yes, every day, except Saturday and Sunday," Laura said. "Well, sometimes on those days, too."

"You don't ever miss a day?" Maurice asked.

"If I'm sick," Laura said. "But I almost never get sick."

"But do you ever just *not* do all that for one day?"

"No, I do it every day. It's my job."

The truth was, Maurice didn't know anyone with a real job. Not the kind of job where you went to the same place every day and did the same thing. That's not how the days unfolded in his world.

"What about you?" Laura asked. "What do you want to be when you grow up?"

Maurice shrugged. "I don't know."

"No? Don't you ever think about it?"

"No," Maurice said without hesitation.

It was the truth. He didn't think about it. He never wondered about his future. He had enough to worry about in the present. That's not something the people in his life worried about either. No one had ever told him it was okay to think about being a fireman, or an astronaut, or a baseball player, or anything like that. He didn't dream about being anything, because he assumed kids like him couldn't have those kinds of dreams.

When Laura finished her milk shake, she and Maurice got up and walked out to the street. It seemed to Maurice that Laura didn't want to say good-bye just yet. If he was being honest, he didn't want to go home yet, either.

As they walked back toward Broadway, Laura asked, "Would you like some ice cream? We can go to Häagen-Dazs. It's right up the street."

"You mean the place with the designer ice cream?" Maurice said.

Maurice didn't get to eat much ice cream, and he'd certainly never had Häagen-Dazs ice cream before, but he'd heard about it and he knew it was considered pretty fancy.

"Designer ice cream?" Laura said. "Yes, I guess it is."

"Can I have a chocolate cone?" he asked.

"Sure," Laura said.

This was more than Maurice could have ever hoped for. He hadn't had a chocolate ice-cream cone in, well, he didn't even know how long. They went in and Laura bought two chocolate cones. They took their ice cream out to the street and ate it as they walked in the afternoon sun. Laura had only had four or five bites by the time Maurice was finished with his. He had chocolate ice cream all over his mouth.

"Is there anything else you want to do today?" Laura said.

Maurice knew just what to ask for.

"Can we go play video games?"

"Sure, why not?"

The arcade was just a couple of blocks down on Broadway. This time Maurice didn't walk behind Laura. He walked right alongside her. He knew he shouldn't be so trusting, but he couldn't help himself. This was fun. This was shaping up to be one of the best days he'd had in a long time. Big Mac, ice cream, and now the arcade—how could he say no to any of those things?

Laura and Maurice walked into the arcade and were hit with a blast of sound—clangs and whistles and bells and laughter and yelling. The arcade was alive with excitement, and the energy filled Maurice with happiness. Kids and teenagers and even adults ran around playing all kinds of video games, joking with each other, horsing around, having a blast. Maurice loved going to the arcade. It was the perfect place to escape from the world for a while.

Laura gave Maurice five quarters, and he ran off to play a game called Asteroids. Maurice dropped the first quarter in and quickly lost himself in the game. He stood on his toes and moved the joystick back and forth. As soon as one game was over, he dropped in another quarter and started playing again. Laura stood a few feet away and watched, a smile on her face, as he won round after round.

When he finished his last game, Maurice shuffled back to Laura. He knew his time for fun was over. They left the arcade and walked up Broadway until they were right back where they met, on the corner of Fifty-Sixth Street. Laura reached into her red purse and pulled out her wallet. She took out a small white card and handed the card to Maurice.

"That's my phone number. If you're ever hungry, please call me," she told him. "I'll make sure you get something to eat."

Maurice looked at the card, then put it in the pocket of his sweatpants.

"Thank you for my lunch and my ice cream and my games," he said. "I had a really great day."

"Me too," Laura said.

Then Maurice turned around and ran back to his apartment. He ran fast. It was almost as if, if he didn't run fast enough, someone might take away what had just happened. Take away the Big Mac and the Häagen-Dazs and the Asteroids. Take it all away, like it hadn't even happened. And Maurice didn't want that. He wanted to remember this day.

When Maurice got back to the Bryant Hotel, he felt really good. The dull ache in his stomach was gone. All that food and ice cream gave him more energy than he'd had in days.

At first he had been worried about going to lunch with Laura, because she was a stranger, and because he had no idea what she wanted from him. He couldn't trust her, because he couldn't trust anyone. That was one of the things that kept him safe on the streets—he never let his guard down. His mother and uncles had taught him to be suspicious of everyone. Maurice built a wall around himself and never let anyone who wasn't family through.

But even so, he had allowed Laura to take him to lunch. He did what he'd always been told not to do. And, to his surprise, it went okay. Nothing bad happened. Laura was really nice. Of course, if he ever told his mother or grandmother about her, they would scold him and tell him to stay away from her, to never be so trusting again. All he could say in his own defense was that sometimes hunger makes you do things you don't want to do.

Maurice ran up to the steps of the Bryant Hotel, but stopped before going in. He reached into his pocket and pulled out the card Laura had given him. It had her name on it—Laura Schroff—and a telephone number.

The truth was, Maurice was *always* hungry, and it wasn't like Laura was *always* going to be there to take him to McDonald's. Besides, a telephone call cost a quarter to make, and Maurice didn't have any extra quarters lying around.

Maurice walked over to the garbage can on the corner of Fifty-Fourth Street, and he threw Laura's card in the trash.

3

TWO DAYS LATER MAURICE woke up hungry again.

When he came out of the dark closet on Thursday morning, he realized he hadn't eaten anything since his lunch with Laura. In those two days his mother came and went, disappearing for hours, then showing up at night and staying up late, laughing with his uncles. Maurice learned that his sisters had eaten the day before when someone cooked something on a hot plate in the apartment. Grilled cheese sandwiches. But because Maurice was out on the street at the time, he didn't get one. There was no such thing as "mealtime" in Maurice's world. No one rang a dinner bell, or called him in when supper was ready. People just ate whenever they could, whenever they got their hands on food. If you weren't there, you missed it. And there were never, ever any leftovers.

Maurice was already old enough to fend for himself. His sisters were older than him, but they were girls, so whenever there was any food around, they usually got it. It was understood that Maurice would be able to find food somehow, because he was almost a man now, even though he was the youngest. He'd found food for himself before, and he would do it again. He had to, or else he wouldn't survive. Once in a while Maurice would tell his mother that he was hungry and ask her for food, but for the most part he had stopped asking. He knew it probably wouldn't do any good.

Now Maurice was starving again. The same dull pain in his stomach. If he focused on it, Maurice could almost taste the Big Mac he'd eaten two days before. He could almost smell the French fries. But thinking about food made the pain even worse, so Maurice tried not to do it.

Maurice stopped thinking about food and thought about what he had to do in order to *get* food. He had to go out on the street again, he had to ask for spare change, and he had to hope that someone as nice as Laura walked by.

He put on his burgundy sweatpants and sweatshirt, slipped into his dirty white sneakers with the broken shoelaces, and did what he always did when he first woke up: counted the people in his apartment. One, two, three . . . eleven. Eleven people, not counting him. Then he kissed his mother on the cheek as she slept, and ran down the filthy hallway.

He stood in his favorite spot and stuck out his hand.

And then he waited.

And waited. And waited.

But no one stopped.

Not in Maurice's first hour on the street, and not in his

second. Or his third. Or fourth. The morning passed and the afternoon came and went, and then it was evening, and the sun started to go down. And, still, Maurice stood there, going on eight hours now. A thousand different people must have passed him by without stopping. Or maybe it was ten thousand. It was a lot. But Maurice stuck it out. He stood in the same spot and kept asking for change. He had no choice. Giving up meant not eating. Maurice kept going.

But no one was stopping. It was one of those bad days. The tight, painful knot in Maurice's stomach grew and grew. His legs felt wobbly. A light rain started to fall as the sun dropped out of sight.

Around seven thirty p.m., after Maurice had been on Fifty-Sixth Street for nearly nine hours, he looked down Broadway and thought he saw a familiar face.

Secretly, he had been hoping that Laura might pass by again. After all, she lived right around the corner. And though he tried not to do it, Maurice couldn't help but look at the faces of the people walking past him, to see if Laura's was among them. Sometimes a woman with brown hair would walk by and Maurice's heart would jump in his chest, but then he would see it wasn't Laura. He tried to forget about her. It wasn't like he could count on her to show up.

Now there were fewer people on the sidewalks because most people were inside somewhere eating dinner. Maurice looked up.

Could it be? Was it her?

And then, in a second, Maurice realized that it *was* her.

It was Laura.

His heart jumped and his stomach flipped. Laura walked right up to him.

"Hi, Maurice!" Laura said cheerily.

"Hello, Miss Laura," Maurice said, his voice sounding like a whisper because he had so little energy. He'd heard people refer to Grandma Rose as "Miss Rose," and he understood it to be a polite way of referring to a lady, so he decided to call Laura *Miss Laura*. She seemed surprised when he said it.

"I was hoping I'd find you here," Laura said. "Well, not hoping. I mean, I wasn't hoping you'd be hungry. I mean . . . well, you know what I mean. Are you hungry?"

"Miss Laura, I'm starving," Maurice said.

"Okay," Laura said. "McDonald's?"

Maurice didn't answer. He just nodded. In his mind, he was already biting into the Big Mac.

At McDonald's, Maurice ordered the same meal he'd ordered two days earlier—Big Mac, French fries, and a chocolate milk shake. He tore into his food again, but halfway through he tried to slow himself down. He didn't want the meal to be over so quickly. He started eating one French fry at a time instead of five. He tried to enjoy every single bite. He tried to stretch the meal out as long as he could.

"Maurice," Laura said as they were eating, "tell me about your family."

"What do you want to know?" Maurice said.

"Well, tell me about your mother."

"Her name's Darcella."

"Okay. And does she work?"

"No, she stays home and she cleans. She vacuums and dusts." This made sense; plenty of moms were stay-at-home moms.

It wasn't true, but Laura wouldn't know that.

"Does she know you're out here?" Laura asked. "On the street, I mean?"

"Nah, she don't care," Maurice said.

Laura seemed shocked by the answer.

"What about your father?" she asked.

"He's not around."

"What happened to him?"

"He's just gone."

Maurice didn't say anything more than that. It wasn't the whole truth, but, again, Laura wouldn't know that. She didn't need to know any more about him or his family, really. Maurice remembered rule number one: *Trust no one.*

And, anyway, Maurice didn't really want to talk about his father. He didn't want to have to even *think* about him.

Maurice knew a few things about his father. He knew them from listening to his mother talk about him. He knew, for instance, that his father was also named Maurice, but that when he was born, no one knew how to spell his name, so it became Morris. He was named after his own father—Maurice's grandfather—which meant that Maurice was the third in a line of Maurice's. If he thought about his father at all, he thought about that—that his father had named him after himself and Maurice's grandfather. And that made Maurice feel good. It made him feel like he was a part of something. Something special.

He also knew that most people didn't call his father Maurice. They called him Lefty, even though he was right handed. This was because, when he would get angry with people, he would knock them out with his left hand.

From everything Maurice had heard, he gathered that his father was a tough man. He wasn't very tall, only five feet two inches, but he was strong and people respected him. Or so his mother said. She explained that Maurice's father had been a part of a street gang called the Tomahawks. The street gang was a group of teenagers who liked to hang out with one another and do things together. If you were part of the gang, everyone else in the gang looked out for you and treated you like a brother. If you weren't in the gang, you were the enemy. That's how the streets worked, his mother told Maurice. The only way not to get hurt by your enemies was to be part of a gang.

Sometimes his mother would talk about the day she met Maurice's father. Darcella grew up surrounded by brothers, and she learned how to fight by being around them, and so she was tough too. So tough that the Tomahawks let her into their street gang. And that's how she met Maurice's father. They liked each other right away. They were both fearless, and they didn't let anyone hurt them. She called him Junebug, which came from the word "Junior," which was part of his official name—Maurice Jr. And he called her Red, which came from "Redbone," which was a nickname for light-skinned African American women like her. They got married and had three children, all before his mother turned twenty. Maurice was the third.

And then, from what Maurice could understand, things turned bad.

From what he could gather, his parents fought a lot. Apparently, they fought all the time. He couldn't remember much, because he was so young when his father walked out. But that's how his mother explained it to him. They were both too tough and too aggressive to be with each other. They weren't a good fit anymore. After a while Maurice's father started disappearing for days at a time, then showing up at their apartment and starting another fight. Sometimes the fighting got so loud, Maurice would run off and hide in the closet. And when he started to cry, his father would tell him to "shut up."

Finally, there was a big fight—the biggest yet. There was a lot of yelling and pushing and arguing. Maurice couldn't remember all of it, but he could still remember how scared he felt. He could remember running to his mother and trying to stop his father from pushing her around. That image would be forever carved into Maurice's memory.

Anyway, the big fight was what ended it all. Some policemen showed up at their apartment, and Maurice's father ran off. This time, he never came back to the apartment. Just like that, he was out of Maurice's life for good.

At McDonald's, Maurice ate his last French fry and took the final sip of his chocolate milk shake. He hated hearing the gurgling sound the straw made, because it meant there was no more left. But he couldn't complain. His stomach was full. He wasn't starving anymore. There were no more pains in his stomach and his head was clear.

Just like last time, Maurice and Laura left McDonald's and walked out onto Eighth Avenue. They walked up toward Broadway and ended up at the same spot where they'd met. Maurice stood there, not wanting to say good-bye.

"Maurice," Laura finally said, "how would you like to get together on Monday night and have dinner again? Except this time, how about if we go someplace different, like the Hard Rock Cafe?"

Maurice could hardly believe it.

The Hard Rock Cafe!? On Fifty-Seventh Street!? He'd walked by it so many times. It was unlike any other place in New York City. It was on the ground floor of a building, and on the outside it had half a car sticking out onto the street! A half of a real car! Almost as if the car had driven straight into the building! And it was so popular that people would line up outside the door just to get in. A big, beefy man at the door would let them in one or two or three at a time, and the rest of the people would keep waiting—sometimes in the cold, sometimes in the rain—until they were let in too. Sometimes they'd wait for hours!

If the place was so popular, Maurice figured, the food had to be *amazing*. But it was more than just the idea of the food that made Maurice curious. The Hard Rock Cafe was a restaurant. He'd never stepped inside such a place before. To Maurice, the Hard Rock Cafe seemed like a magical wonderland.

When he'd walk by, Maurice would try to look inside when people came in or out, and every time the door swung open the sound of music would drift out, and the people leaving or going in were always laughing, so happy, so *excited*; Maurice wanted to experience that too. He wanted to see beyond the revolving door. He wanted to be part of the wonderland!

But, of course, he couldn't go in. The Hard Rock Cafe was off limits if you didn't have any money. His only hope of ever getting inside was somehow sneaking in, just to look around, but even that was impossible because of the big, beefy man stationed right outside. No, the Hard Rock Cafe was not a place for him. It was not a place for the *us*.

It was a place for *them*.

Except now, Laura was offering to take Maurice there. To take him *inside*.

When Laura made the offer, Maurice wanted to scream, *Yes, yes, please!* Instead, he just said, "Okay."

Then he asked, "Can I wear these clothes?"

Maurice knew his sweatpants and sweatshirt were dirty. He'd seen the kinds of people who went into the Hard Rock

Cafe; they did not wear dirty clothes. But he had no other options. He hoped it was okay.

"Yes, you can," Laura said. "How about if we meet right here on Monday, at seven o'clock, okay?"

"Yes, Miss Laura," Maurice said. "And thank you for my meal."

"You're welcome, Maurice."

And then Maurice ran off again, back to the Bryant Hotel, his mind racing with what it would be like to go to the Hard Rock Cafe, what he would order, and how great it would be—but also racing with the worry that he was breaking rule number one again.

No one does nothing for nothing. So don't trust no one.

Why was Laura being so nice to him? What did she want from him? *No one does nothing for nothing,* so why was she doing these things? And why was he letting her be so nice to him? Why was he trusting her?

Back in his family's small apartment, Maurice curled up in the closet. Only this time, his stomach was full, and the closet didn't feel so spooky anymore. Maurice fell into a deep sleep and dreamed about a half car sticking out of a building, and the sight of it was so silly, so funny, that it made him laugh, and laugh and laugh.

4

THE NEXT MORNING MAURICE woke to the sound of someone banging on the door of the apartment. It was a loud, jarring sound.

"Open up!" he heard a man yelling. "Come on, open up!"

Maurice didn't like it when people knocked on the door. In his experience, someone knocking on the door *always* meant bad news. He remembered the time, a few years before he met Laura, when he was staying with his mother, sisters, and grandmother in a different one-room apartment in New York City. He thought back to what happened on that day when he opened the front door.

On that day, he was alone in the apartment with Grandma Rose. She was in her chair, and she was either asleep or she had her eyes closed and was ignoring the knocking on the door. But whoever it was kept banging loudly.

"Come on, open up!" some other man yelled. "Let's go, open up."

Maurice knew that if he didn't answer, eventually the men would break the door down. He crept slowly toward the closed door and talked to the men through it.

"What do you want?" Maurice yelled.

"We need to talk to you," the man said. "Please, open up."

Maurice knew something bad was about to happen. He looked at the window in the apartment. He thought of opening it and crawling out on the ledge and escaping. He went over and opened the window and looked down at the sidewalk. The apartment was on the fifth floor. It was a long drop down. Maurice closed the window. He wouldn't be able to escape that way.

"Come on!" yelled the first man again.

And in an instant Maurice hatched a plan.

He went to the front door and opened it. Then he jumped outside and quickly closed the door behind him. That way, the men couldn't get in and bother Grandma Rose.

Maurice looked up at the two men who stood there towering over him. They were both around his mother's age, and they were wearing dark suits. One was kind of heavy, the other one had a bushy mustache.

"Who else is in there?" the heavy one asked.

"No one," Maurice said. "It's just me."

"What's your name?"

"Maurice."

"We're from the Bureau of Child Welfare," Mustache said. "We need to take you down to the lobby."

Maurice went with the men. They walked him down the

stairs, one on either side of him. In the lobby, they stopped so Heavy could make a phone call. Mustache stood next to Maurice and put his hand on his shoulder. His grip was tight.

Maurice just stood there and waited. He waited for his moment. He listened as Heavy made his phone call and said something to someone, and then he watched as Mustache took a pack of cigarettes out of his pocket. Mustache took his hand off Maurice's shoulder to reach for the lighter in his other pocket. Maurice waited until the man flicked the lighter on and lit his cigarette. Just before Mustache slipped the lighter back into his pocket, Maurice made his move.

He bolted, racing out of the lobby like he was shot out of a cannon—down the steps, into the street. Thank goodness he knew every corner, every turn. This was the reason why he paid so much attention to his surroundings. He always needed to have an escape route.

"Get back here!" he heard Mustache yell. "Stop that boy!"

Maurice ran down his street, toward Broadway. He looked over his shoulder and saw the two men get into a white van that was parked outside the building where he lived. He kept running, and when he looked over his shoulder again, the van was on the move. He could hear the screech of tires as it drove speedily toward him.

When he got to Broadway, Maurice turned and kept running as fast as he could. The traffic was heavy, and Maurice hoped the van wouldn't be able to catch up to him. He made it three blocks without stopping, dodging people, swerving around fire hydrants, before he stopped to look around. He couldn't see the white van anywhere.

All of a sudden, he heard the screech of tires again. It was the white van, heading straight for him.

Maurice took off. This time he ran from Broadway to Eighth Avenue. Then he turned and ran uptown. He didn't stop until he'd run ten whole blocks. When he finally slowed down, he was out of breath. He looked around but couldn't see a white van anywhere. He sat down on the sidewalk for a moment, just to catch his breath.

Then he heard the screech of tires again.

It couldn't be. How could they still be following him? Apparently, Maurice wasn't as invisible as he thought. He got up and started to run again, but the van was going fast, and before he knew it, the van was only thirty feet behind him. Maurice quickly turned a corner and dived under a parked car. He was small and thin enough that he was able to roll right under it. He watched as the white van drove right past his hiding spot.

But then, just a hundred or so feet up the block, the white van stopped. Maurice watched as the doors flew open, and Heavy and Mustache stepped out. He watched as they started walking in his direction.

Maurice held his breath. Had they seen him dive under the car? Maurice's instinct was to get up and run, but he stayed still and watched as the men got closer. They got close enough for him to see their shoes. One of them wore brown shoes with black socks. The other wore black shoes with white socks.

Now the shoes were just a few feet away. Slowly, deliberately, they kept coming. Clop, clop, clop. Maurice held his breath as the shoes walked by him and kept going. Maurice didn't dare move a muscle until their shoes were out of sight.

They had missed him!

Just as he was about to inch out from under the car, he heard them again. They had turned around! Back toward him.

Maurice saw one of the shoes disappear behind a knee. Two hands, a face. It was Heavy. And Heavy saw Maurice.

"There he is!"

Maurice rolled out from under the car and took off again. The men scrambled back into the van. Maurice ran and ran and ran and headed to the only place he could think of to go.

Back to his family.

Maurice ran into his building, up the stairs, and down the hallway. When he got to his apartment, the door was locked. He banged on the door and yelled.

"Let me in, it's Maurice, let me in, they chasing me!"

The door opened just as Mustache and Heavy were barreling down the hallway. Maurice looked up to see who had opened it.

It was Grandma Rose.

Maurice lunged at her and held on to her waist.

Heavy and Mustache stopped running and walked up to the apartment. They were breathing very loudly, especially Heavy.

"We're from the Bureau of Child Welfare," Mustache told Grandma Rose. "This boy's mother has been incarcerated, and we need to take him with us."

Mustache had to be a full foot taller than Grandma Rose and a hundred pounds heavier. He had an angry look on his face, and he clearly meant business. He wasn't asking permission to take Maurice. He was explaining how things were going to go.

But Grandma Rose had other ideas.

"This child ain't going nowhere," she said matter-of-factly.

Then she pulled Maurice into the apartment and slammed the door shut with a loud bang.

Maurice waited for the men to start pounding on the door and yelling again. But they didn't. All he heard was silence. Maybe the men were too tired from all that running. Or maybe Grandma Rose had scared them

Whatever it was that made them change their minds, the men thankfully went away.

Now, years later, someone was banging on his front door again. Grandma Rose, same as before, was asleep in her chair. Maurice's two sisters were also asleep on the bed. Maurice noticed that his mother wasn't there.

He went to the door and opened it. Two men in suits were standing there.

"Who are you?" one of the men asked Maurice.

"Who are *you*?" Maurice asked back.

"We're from the Bureau of Child Welfare," the man said.

And then he said a few more things. After a while, Maurice stopped listening. He had heard his mother's name, and he heard the word "incarcerated."

He knew what it meant. He'd heard it before. It meant his mother was in jail.

The idea of his mother being arrested and put in jail should have frightened him, but it didn't. It had happened before. No one ever explained to Maurice why his mother was arrested. No one acted like it was a big deal. Whenever it happened, everyone just went on with their lives, and a day or two later, Maurice's mother would show up at the apartment, as if nothing had happened. She never explained anything to Maurice then, either, but he was always so happy to see her again. For all he knew, everyone's parents got arrested every now and then.

And so, the next morning Maurice woke up, walked out of the closet, and counted the people in the apartment. One, two, three . . . eight. Eight people.

One of them was his mother.

For once, Maurice didn't mind the big crowd in his room that morning, because it included his mother.

5

WHEN MONDAY CAME AROUND, Maurice was more excited than he had been in a long time. Maybe ever. He didn't tell his mother or his sisters or Grandma Rose that he was going to meet Laura. He didn't have to. No one was going to ask him where he was going. He hadn't mentioned Laura to anyone, and he didn't plan to. He didn't feel bad about not telling them, because he knew what his family would say if he did. They would tell him to stop talking to her. *She wants something from you*, they'd say. *She wants to take you away from us.*

Maurice didn't tell anyone he was going to the Hard Rock Cafe. Part of him wanted to tell *someone* about the cool place he was going to, but he didn't. The day before, though, he decided to wash his sweatpants and sweatshirt because they were really dirty. Maurice took a raggedy, worn-out towel that he found in the corner of the room, and went down to the basement of the Bryant. He had no soap to wash his clothes with, but he figured that was okay. At least he could scrub them in some warm water. When he got to the laundry room, he was relieved no one else was there.

Maurice quickly took of his clothes and wrapped the towel around himself. Then he began to scrub his sweatpants and sweatshirt in the large laundry sink.

Twenty minutes later he did his best to wring the clothes dry. Then he took them back to his family's room and laid them out on the slightly warm radiator. He felt confident they would be dry by the next day. Meanwhile, he took his sneakers into the closet and tried to wipe off all the dirt with a sock he found on the floor.

No one asked why he suddenly needed clean clothes and shiny sneakers. No one seemed to notice.

On Monday evening Maurice put on his nearly dry, nearly clean clothes and his slightly less scruffy white sneakers (shoelaces still broken), and he slipped out of the apartment. When he got to his spot on the corner of Fifty-Sixth Street, five minutes after seven p.m., Laura was already there.

"Hi, Maurice," she said.

"Hi, Miss Laura."

"Wow, you look nice," Laura said with a smile.

"It's just the same stuff I always wear," Maurice said.

Together, they walked uptown one block to Fifty-Seventh Street, then turned the corner and headed west. Within minutes they were outside the Hard Rock Cafe. There it was, right in front of Maurice. Wonderland. The half a car sticking out of the wall. The line of people. The big, beefy guy at the door. The sound of the music playing inside.

"Come on," Laura said, "we don't have to wait in line. We have a reservation."

Maurice didn't know what a reservation was. But it didn't matter. He followed Laura as she walked to the front of the line and said something to the big, beefy man. He opened the door, and Laura walked in. Maurice hesitated for a moment as the big, beefy man looked down at him. Maurice had seen that look before. *This place isn't for you. You don't belong here.*

"Come on, Maurice," Laura said, motioning for him to follow, and Maurice did. He walked past the big, beefy man, who kept looking at him in that harsh way, and entered the Hard Rock Cafe.

It was spectacular. It was crazy. It was *exciting*. Most of all, it was loud. Really loud. Rock music blared from a number of speakers all around the restaurant, and when Laura turned and said something to him, Maurice couldn't even hear her. The restaurant was dark, but there were neon signs everywhere, and on the walls Maurice saw real guitars and posters of people playing them. All the tables were filled with people, and all the people were talking and laughing and eating. It was like the arcade, only noisier and happier.

Plus, there was the food.

Maurice smelled it before he saw it. Men and women carrying big trays swept past him as he walked behind Laura. Maurice watched as they set the trays down near a table. On each tray, there were six or seven plates heaped with food.

Hamburgers. French fries. Sandwiches. Bowls of ice cream. Big glasses filled with soda. Plates and plates and plates. Maurice had never seen—or smelled—anything like it.

Finally, Laura and Maurice arrived at a small table near the back of the restaurant. Laura motioned for Maurice to sit down, and he hopped up into his chair. It felt funny. He looked down and saw that the chair was padded with something. Almost like he was sitting on a pillow. It felt comfortable. It felt good. It wasn't like any chair Maurice had ever sat in before.

A woman came over and handed something to Maurice. She handed the same thing to Laura. It was several pages, and it had pictures of food on it.

"Hi, I'm Janice, and I'll be your waitress tonight," she said. "Here are your menus; let me know if you have any questions," the woman said.

Maurice didn't know what a menu was.

But he did know what a steak was, and he knew what it looked like. And on one of the pages of the "menu," Maurice saw a picture of a big, beautiful steak. He'd never eaten one before, but he had heard one of his uncles talk about eating a steak, and about how thick and juicy and delicious it was. *Better than hamburgers?* Maurice had asked. *Much better, little man,* his uncle had said.

Now here was Maurice's chance to have a steak of his own.

"Miss Laura, can I have a steak with mashed potatoes?" he asked.

"You can have anything you want," Laura answered.

"Okay, I'll have steak," Maurice said.

When the waitress came back, Laura asked her for steak and mashed potatoes for Maurice, and ordered the same thing for herself. She also ordered two Diet Cokes. Maurice looked around the restaurant and tried to take it all in. People come to your table and ask you what you want to eat? And then they bring it to you? And you can choose from a list of hundreds of different kinds of food? Maurice had suspected the Hard Rock Cafe was a magical wonderland, but it was even better than he'd expected. His imagination didn't stretch far enough to include anything like this. Maurice had always known that there was *us* and there was *them*. And he knew that those two worlds were very different.

But he hadn't really understood *how* different until that moment.

Before long, a man came up and put two big knives down on the table, one in front of Maurice, one in front of Laura. Maurice had seen his share of knives before—sometimes his uncles carried them, and even his grandma, Rose, had a box cutter she kept hidden in her chair—but he'd never seen a knife with such a big sharp blade and such a thick wooden handle.

"That's a steak knife," Laura said, without him asking. She must have noticed him looking at it, wondering why it was there. "It's a special knife that cuts through steaks so you can easily cut off pieces to eat."

Just then the waitress returned. She was carrying two

LAURA SCHROFF

plates, one in each hand. She put one plate down in front of
Laura, and the other in front of Maurice. When he finally got a
look at his plate, he could hardly believe it.

The steak was *huge*.

It was probably the size of four McDonald's hamburgers
smashed together. No, five hamburgers. Maybe six. And next
to it was a pile of creamy-white mashed potatoes as big as three
scoops of ice cream. Three giant scoops. It was the most food
Maurice had ever had in front of him in his entire life. And to
top it all off, the waitress set down a tall glass of Diet Coke and
ice filled to the very brim.

"Well, what do you think?" Laura asked. "Looks pretty
good, doesn't it?"

Maurice was speechless. The food didn't just look good to
him. It looked like a miracle.

Maurice watched as Laura took her steak knife in one hand
and her fork in the other and began to slice the steak. Hesi-
tantly, Maurice picked up his own steak knife. It was so big,
it barely fit in his hand. He picked up his fork with the other
hand, and then he looked at his steak. He honestly didn't know
what to do next. He'd handled a knife and fork before, here
and there, though usually he ate fast food that didn't require a
fork or spoon or knife. But he'd never had to deal with a knife
this big before, or, for that matter, with a steak this size.

As best he could, Maurice tried to cut a piece off one end
of his steak. He watched for how Laura did it, and he tried to
copy her. But she cut her steak so quickly and so effortlessly, it

44

was hard to figure out how she did it. When Maurice pushed down with his knife, it didn't cut through the steak at all. But he kept trying. More than anything in the world, he wanted to get a piece of the steak in his mouth. He wanted to taste it and make the pain in his stomach start to go away. He kept struggling with the knife and fork, trying to cut off a piece.

Laura watched him as he struggled. Once or twice it looked like she wanted to say something, or to show him how to do it, but she didn't. She just let him work at it. Maybe she didn't want to embarrass him by showing him how to properly use a knife and fork in front of all these other people. But even so, Maurice could tell that Laura wanted to help him somehow, so he could start eating at last.

Finally, Laura said, "Back and forth, like this," and she used her knife to cut through the meat.

Maurice watched and tried to copy her actions. He moved his knife back and forth and felt it start to cut through the steak. It took him a few seconds, but finally he detached a jagged chunk of steak that he could pick up with his fork and put into his mouth.

When he did, he knew instantly that his uncle was right. It was the very best thing he had ever tasted in his life. Better than hamburgers, better than Häagen-Dazs, better than *anything*.

It took Maurice a long time to cut through the whole steak, which was good because it made him slow down, and it made the meal last longer. Laura asked him a few questions while they ate—about his friends, his life, the kinds of things he liked doing. To Maurice, it didn't seem like she was being nosy; it seemed like she was asking questions just to be friendly. Still, Maurice answered some of them with the truth, and some of them with little white lies. There was still no reason for him to tell her everything about his life. He wasn't completely sure what was going on; he felt deep down that she had to want *something*, because, after all, *no one does nothing for nothing*. And as long as he couldn't figure out what it was that she wanted, he had to be careful. He had to keep her behind the wall he'd built around himself.

When the meal was over, and Maurice was fuller than he'd ever been, they walked out onto Fifty-Seventh Street, back to their meeting spot. When they got there, Laura turned and faced Maurice.

"Maurice, would you like to meet again next Monday and have dinner with me?" she asked.

"Yes, I would like that," he said.

"Maybe we can make this a habit," Laura said. "You know, meeting on Mondays. Would that be okay?"

"Yes," Maurice replied.

"Okay, then. We'll meet right here next Monday. Seven o'clock?"

"Okay, Miss Laura. And thank you for my steak."

Maurice turned and ran back home. He ran into the Bryant and up the stairs and down the hallway to his apartment. When he got inside, he saw his sisters, Celeste and LaToya, playing together on the bed. Grandma Rose was in her chair, and his aunt and cousins were fast asleep on the other bed. His mother and uncles were gone. Maurice hopped onto the bed with his sisters.

"You guys hungry?" he asked them.

Both Celeste and LaToya nodded their heads.

Maurice reached into the pocket of his sweatpants and pulled out a napkin that was wrapped around something. He unfolded the napkin; inside were two big pieces of steak. At the Hard Rock Cafe, when Laura wasn't watching, Maurice had slipped the pieces into a napkin and put them in his pocket. The pieces weren't hot anymore, but they still looked delicious. Maurice handed the steak to his sisters. He watched as they bit into it and smiled.

Maurice smiled too.

6

MAURICE BEGAN TO BUILD his weeks around Mondays. There were six other days of the week that went on pretty much like they always did—and then there was Monday. Monday was different. Monday was special now. Monday was the day when Maurice would meet Laura on Fifty-Sixth Street, and the two of them would have a great dinner somewhere. It was the only day of the week when Maurice could be certain he would get something to eat.

When Monday finally rolled around, Maurice got ready to meet Laura at seven o'clock, as they'd planned. His mother and uncles weren't around, but Grandma Rose was. She was in her chair with her eyes closed, as usual. But before Maurice had the chance to slip out the front door, Grandma Rose opened her eyes and called out to him.

"Maurice, get back here," she said.

Maurice did as he was told.

"Where you off to?" Rose asked.

Maurice still hadn't mentioned Laura to anyone in his family, and he didn't want to have to mention her now.

"Out," he said.

"Out where?"

"Just out," Maurice replied.

"Child, you listen to me," Rose said. "You tell me where you goin', or you ain't goin' nowhere, understood?"

Maurice didn't dare lie to Grandma Rose. Not telling her the full truth was one thing. But lying? No, he couldn't do that.

"There's this lady," Maurice said.

"What lady?"

"Some lady I met on the corner."

"What you mean, some lady? What does she want with you?"

"Nothing," Maurice said. "She just buys me food."

Grandma Rose sat up in her chair and leaned forward. Her eyes got narrow and hard.

"What does she want from you in exchange for buyin' you food?"

"Nothing," Maurice said.

"She gotta want something," Rose said. "Everyone's got an angle. Everyone's working something. Don't be foolish, child. What is she after?"

"I don't know," Maurice finally said. "Maybe she's just nice."

Grandma Rose reached out and grabbed Maurice by his skinny arm. Her grip was strong, much stronger than you'd think from looking at her.

"Maurice, this lady ain't your friend," she said. "Nobody's just nice. She wants to take you away from your family. She wants to take you somewhere so we never see you again. Is that what you want?"

"No, ma'am," Maurice said.

"Then why you being so foolish and runnin' off to meet her?"

Maurice thought about it for a moment.

"'Cause I'm hungry," he finally said.

Grandma Rose let go of his arm. She was quiet for a moment, almost like she couldn't think what to say in response.

"Just be careful," she finally said. "This lady may be nice, but she ain't your family. Your family is all you got, you hear me?"

"Yes, ma'am," Maurice said. "You're not gonna tell Momma about the lady, are you?"

"Not yet," Rose said. "So long as you remember what I'm sayin'. Whoever this lady is, she lives in a different world. It's a world where we don't fit. You start tryin' to live in her world, you'll get soft. And if you get soft, you'll get hurt. In our world, you gotta stay hard, you hear me?"

Maurice listened to what his grandmother told him. He understood what she was trying to do. She was trying to protect him. She was saying that Laura might well be a nice lady and all, but she doesn't understand our world. She'll never understand it, and she doesn't care about it, either.

She doesn't really care about you, Maurice.

Maurice took his grandmother's words seriously. She had survived the streets for a long, long time. And if he wanted to survive too, he ought to listen to her. What's more, he knew she loved him. She wasn't working any scheme. She was his blood, and she wanted to protect him. She wanted him to learn what he needed in order to survive.

"Now get on over here and give me a kiss," Rose said.

Maurice leaned forward and kissed Grandma Rose on the cheek.

When Maurice got to his customary spot, Laura was already there.

"Hi, Maurice," she said with a smile.

"Hi, Miss Laura."

"Maurice, I have an idea. What if, instead of going to a restaurant tonight, we go to my apartment and I'll make you a home-cooked dinner? Would you like that?"

The idea of a home-cooked meal was thrilling. Maurice had vague memories of when his mother cooked big dinners for him and his sisters, years and years ago, and he could almost remember how delicious they had been.

But still—having a home-cooked dinner meant he had to go with Laura to her apartment in the Symphony. And what had Grandma Rose just told him about straying out of his world and into her world? Hadn't she just warned him to be careful—to be less trusting?

What if Laura was leading him into some kind of trap?

"I can make roasted chicken with mashed potatoes," she said. "And for dessert, we can bake chocolate chip cookies."

Maurice didn't answer Laura right away, but deep down he already knew what his answer would be. He felt that dull, painful ache in his stomach again. He was so hungry and this was a sure meal. He pictured roasted chicken and mashed potatoes in his mind and it made him so happy, he had to stop himself from smiling.

Yes, he would be careful. He would keep up his guard. He would stay behind the big brick wall he had built around himself.

But his answer would be yes.

"I would like that," Maurice finally said.

"Great!" Laura said. "Okay, then, let's go."

Together, Maurice and Laura turned the corner of Fifty-Sixth Street and headed to the lobby of the Symphony building.

It felt strange for Maurice to walk through the revolving doors that led into the lobby. He was so accustomed to walking past the building and getting dirty looks from the tenants and the man in the gray suit and cap who stood in the lobby or outside on the street, shooing away people who didn't belong there. The Symphony's revolving door was like the front door to the Hard Rock Cafe—a passageway into another universe. A universe where people like Maurice simply weren't welcome.

This time, however, no one shooed him away. Maurice

walked into the lobby and looked around. It was gigantic. It was the size of about ten of his apartments put together. The ceilings were really high and the floor was so shiny, it glistened. It was hard for Maurice to imagine that nobody actually lived in the lobby—that a place this big and this beautiful was just a place for people to *pass through*.

Maurice followed Laura as she walked toward the elevators in the back. Standing near the elevator was the man in the gray suit and cap—the man who kept unwanted visitors away.

"Hi, Steve, how are you tonight?" Laura asked him.

"I'm great, Miss Schroff. How are you?" the man said.

"Not too bad."

Then the man in the suit and cap looked down at Maurice. The man was tall and stocky, looked to be in his thirties, like Laura. When he glanced down at Maurice, the smile on his face disappeared.

"Steve, this is my friend Maurice," Laura said.

"Well, hello, Maurice, pleased to meet you," the man said, putting out his hand for Maurice to shake.

Maurice reached out and the two shook hands. Maurice's hand felt as if it was being crushed by Steve's strong grip. As always, Maurice tried to size Steve up. *Is he a threat?* The answer was pretty obvious. The look on Steve's face revealed that he simply couldn't figure out what Laura was doing with someone like him. For sure, Steve recognized Maurice as the kid standing out on Fifty-Sixth Street. For sure, he knew that Maurice was a street kid. What did Laura mean when she said "my friend"? How could she possibly be friends with someone like Maurice?

Maurice pulled his hand out of Steve's grip and looked away.

"Well, have a nice evening, Ms. Schroff," Steve said. "And you too, *Maurice*." He said his name in a way that made it sound like a bad word. Maurice understood it was Steve's way of letting him know that he wasn't fooling him. Maybe Laura didn't care that he was a street kid, but Steve sure did. It was Steve's job to keep street kids away from the tenants. Steve's expression let Maurice know that he would be keeping his eye on him.

When Laura walked into the elevator ahead of Maurice, her back turned to him, Maurice peered over his shoulder and looked straight at Steve. Then he gave him a look.

Maurice hoped that the look said, *Don't mess with me.*

Then Maurice jumped into the elevator.

A few of the places where Maurice had lived had working elevators, but most of them didn't. And the ones that did work didn't look *anything* like the elevator in Laura's building. Just the elevator was about half the size of Maurice's apartment. The walls were made of wood that was polished and shiny, and when the elevator opened on Laura's floor, it opened onto a hallway that had a plush carpet covering the whole floor. Everything in the Symphony looked brand new.

Then they arrived at Laura's apartment.

It wasn't all that big—probably just three times the size

of Maurice's apartment. But it was beautiful. It had big windows that went from the floor to the ceiling, and it had a door that led out onto a balcony. The walls were painted a soft blue color. Off to the side was a kitchen that was filled with new appliances. In the main room there was a big wooden dresser, and a big wooden table with two chairs around it, and a really nice looking sofa. There was also a huge piece of furniture— Maurice had no idea what it was used for—that looked really old but wasn't beat up or broken down. Later on, he would hear Laura refer to it as an "antique," whatever that meant.

At the very end of the large room was Laura's bed, which had a big fluffy cover and lots and lots of pillows. A television and a VCR were on a table that faced the bed.

More than anything, Maurice thought, Laura's apartment looked *comfortable*.

For sure, it wasn't like any home Maurice had ever been in before.

"Well, here it is," Laura said. "My apartment. What do you think?"

"It's great," Maurice said. He made a point of standing in a spot that had a clear, straight path to the front door, in case he had to run.

"Well, look around, make yourself at home," Laura said. "I'll be right back."

Suddenly, a little gray cat ran up to Maurice.

"Oh, that's Jodie," Laura said. She picked Jodie up, gave her a quick kiss, and handed her to Maurice.

"She loves to be held," Laura said.

When Laura left, Maurice looked around the apartment some more. There were so many little things to look at. So many *possessions*. Books. Pictures. Lamps. A CD player on a shelf. A pretty clock that looked old.

Then Maurice saw something that he had to look at twice before he could believe it was real.

It was a jug made of plastic, sitting on the floor. It was one of those big water jugs that was about the size of a suitcase. And inside the jug there were coins. Pennies, nickels, dimes, quarters. And not just a few coins.

No—the jug was almost filled to the very top with coins.

For Maurice, it was the most amazing sight. So many days Maurice stood on a street corner for ten hours hoping to end up with maybe five or six or ten coins in his pocket. And those few coins would be gone before he went back home. In his whole life, he'd never seen more than a handful of coins in any one place at any one time.

And there, right in front of him, were *thousands and thousands of coins*! More coins than he could imagine even in his craziest dreams! Enough coins to buy a Big Mac, French fries, and Diet Coke every day for a year, or maybe five years!

Wow, Maurice thought. *Laura is rich! She has all this money in a jug and she's not even spending it!* It was a display of wealth and treasure that truly dazzled Maurice, and without realizing it, he took a few steps closer to the jug. He got close enough to reach right in and scoop up a handful of beautiful silver coins.

Just then Laura came back into the living room and saw Maurice standing near the jug.

"Maurice," she said, "I want us to have a serious conversation about something, and it's a conversation we're only going to have one time."

Maurice froze in his spot. He felt like he was in trouble somehow.

"Let's sit down over here," Laura said.

Maurice followed her to the sofa and waited for her to sit. When she did, he sat as far away from her as he possibly could. Then he waited to hear what Laura had to say.

This is it, he thought. *I'm finally going to find out what she wants.*

"Maurice, the reason I invited you to my apartment is because I consider you my friend," she said. "Friendship is built on trust, and I want you to know that I will never betray that trust. I also want you to know that if anything is ever missing from my apartment, we won't be friends anymore."

When Laura used the word "trust," Maurice had only one thought running through his mind—*trust no one, trust no one, trust no one.*

"Seriously, I want you to know that you will always be able to trust me," Laura went on. "But in a friendship, trust runs both ways. I have to be able to trust you, too. Do you understand?"

"Yes, Miss Laura," Maurice said.

Then he waited for what came next.

The *real* reason why he was there.

But, much to his surprise, Laura had stopped talking. She didn't say anything else. There wasn't more coming. That was her whole speech.

"Is that it?" Maurice finally asked. "That's all you want? You just want to be my friend?"

"Well, yes, of course," Laura said.

Maurice felt himself relax. Again and again, the adults in his life had told him not to trust anyone. They'd convinced him it was the most dangerous thing he could do. But now, as he sat next to Laura, something inside Maurice told him that trusting her wouldn't be all that dangerous. Something made him think that trusting her would be *okay*. He'd never felt anything like that for anyone who wasn't in his family. He'd never felt he could trust anyone that wasn't one of *us*. But this felt different. Laura asked him to be her friend, and for some reason, he believed that's all she wanted. He believed they *could* be friends. And what was so wrong with that?

Was it possible that, in at least this one instance, *no one does nothing for nothing* wasn't true?

Maurice stood up and stuck out his hand, just as he'd seen Steve do in the lobby. Laura got up too.

"A deal's a deal," Maurice said, and they shook on it.

"A deal's a deal," Laura said in reply. "Now let's have dinner."

7

THE SMELL OF CHICKEN hit him right away. It was overwhelming. It smelled so good, Maurice could almost taste it.

"The chicken should be ready soon; I'm going to heat up the mashed potatoes," Laura said. "Meanwhile, can you please set the dinner table, Maurice?"

Laura handed him two white plates with two forks, two knives, and two napkins on top, and pointed toward the table in the main room.

Maurice didn't know what she meant. But Laura was already busy doing something else. Maurice took the two plates to the dinner table.

He put them down and took the top plate off and set it next to the other plate. Then he took the forks and knives and put them next to the two plates. He took the napkins and put them next to the forks and knives. Everything was set up in a row on one side of the table.

There, Maurice thought. *The table's set.*

While Laura kept working in the kitchen—and the smell of roasted chicken got stronger and stronger—Maurice looked around the apartment some more. He noticed there wasn't a single messy spot in the whole place. No shoes lying around, no stray shirts or pants, no empty soda bottles. Maurice walked over to the wooden dresser and looked at some of the framed photos on top of it. One of them showed Laura with some other people about her age, laughing and hugging. Another photo showed Laura as a teenager. She looked pretty much the same, except a lot younger.

Then Maurice noticed a small photo in a silver frame. The photo showed five children sitting in front of a Christmas tree. There were three girls and two boys. Some of the children looked older than Maurice and one was a baby, too. One of the girls, Maurice noticed, had a smile that looked a lot like Laura's smile. When he looked closer, he realized it *was* Laura, from when she was about the same age as him.

Which meant the children she was with were probably her brothers and sisters. Maurice reached out and carefully picked up the silver frame so he could see the photo up close. It was cool to see what Laura looked like when she was younger. And it was nice to see how happy she looked in the photo. How happy *all* the kids looked. They were smiling, even the baby, and they all had wrapped Christmas presents in front of them, and to Maurice it looked like the most wonderful moment he could imagine. No wonder Laura kept this photo in her apartment. Who wouldn't want to remember her childhood when it had been so happy?

What Maurice didn't realize, as he held the framed photo in his hand, was that it told a different story from the one he had imagined in his mind.

The photo held the answer to the question that had so puzzled Maurice—why was Laura being so kind to him?

It was only much, much later, when Laura would share a story with him about her brother Frankie that Maurice's question was finally answered.

Frankie loved baseball. He played in the town's Little League and in his backyard with his brother and sisters. Frankie's favorite possession in the world was his baseball glove, a worn leather Rawlings mitt his mother bought for him. There was nothing in the world Frankie liked doing more than playing catch in the yard—and nothing in the world more meaningful to him than his beautiful baseball glove.

One day Frankie and his two sisters Laura and Annette were playing in the living room of their family's small, brick, ranch-style home in Huntington Station, a quiet neighborhood on New York's Long Island. Laura's father, Nunzie, had built the house himself. On that day their mother, Marie, wasn't home—she was working as a waitress at the Huntington Town House. Nunzie wasn't home either—he worked as a builder during the day, and at night he worked as a bartender.

Laura and Annette were running around, playing tag. Frankie was off by himself, fooling around with one of his father's tools, a tape measure. Down the hall from the living room, Laura's baby sister, Nancy, was asleep in her crib.

Suddenly, the children heard the loud screech of tires in the driveway outside their home. They all stopped what they were doing and froze. They knew what that screeching meant. Their father was home.

"Quick, close the windows!" Laura yelled out, and Annette ran around shutting all the windows in the living room. Their mother had taught them to always close the windows when their father came home, so that the neighbors wouldn't hear anything when the fighting started.

Laura's father, Nunzie, had a sickness too. His sickness happened when he drank too much alcohol. When he drank too much, Nunzie would go from being a happy, loving, wonderful man to someone who was angry and mean, most of the time about nothing at all. And when Nunzie got angry, he could be scary. He would yell a lot and maybe knock things over and sometimes break things. He would turn into a completely different person.

When the children heard the sound, they knew it was their father coming home from work. The screeching meant he was driving too fast.

And driving too fast meant he was angry.

While Annette and Laura ran around shutting all the windows, Frankie ran to his bedroom to hide. Along the way, Frankie dropped the tape measure he'd been playing with.

The front door swung open. Laura and Annette ran into the bedroom they shared as well. Frankie hid in his closet and tried to be as still as possible. Meanwhile, Nunzie walked through the living room.

"Hello?!" he yelled out. "Where is everybody?"

His voice was hard and loud. He was ready to pick a fight.

Then Nunzie spotted something on the floor. He bent down and picked it up. It was his tape measure.

And it was broken.

"Frankie!" he screamed. "What did I tell you about playing with my tools!

"FRANKIE!"

From their bedrooms the children could hear their father ranting. They could hear the stomping sound of Nunzie charging down the hallway toward Frankie's bedroom.

Frankie could tell when his father finally walked into the bedroom.

"I know you're here somewhere," Nunzie yelled. "You'd better not be hiding from me!"

A loud crash echoed down the hallway. Then another, and another. Nunzie was throwing things around. He was tearing Frankie's bedroom apart. In the closet, Frankie began to quietly cry. Laura and Annette were crying too. They didn't know what to do.

"If you won't come out," Nunzie yelled, "I guess I'll have to take your baseball glove to make up for the tool you broke."

When Laura heard her father say that, she and Annette ran out of their bedroom and into Frankie's room. They begged their father to stop.

But Nunzie didn't listen. He wanted to punish Frankie for breaking his tape measure.

Frankie ran out of his closet.

"Not my glove!" he yelled at his father. "Please, Dad, not my glove!"

All the children chased after Nunzie as he marched down the hallway with Frankie's baseball mitt in his hand. Frankie kept crying and pleading. They ran after Nunzie through the living room and through the front door, all the way to the garage.

"No, Dad, no!" Frankie screamed. "Please, Dad, no!"

But Nunzie wasn't listening. Nothing could stop him now.

Laura and Annette caught up with Frankie and held on to him to keep him from getting any closer to their father. Together they all watched as Nunzie grabbed the shearing scissors from off a hook in his garage tool station. The scissors were huge and very sharp.

"You break my tools, I destroy your glove," Nunzie said, before cutting into the leather of the glove with the garden shears.

"NO, DAD, NO!" Frankie yelled.

It was too late. Nunzie was cutting Frankie's glove into pieces. One by one, ragged chunks of leather fell to the ground. Frankie couldn't bear to watch it any longer, so he broke away from Laura and Annette and ran back into the house. His sisters ran after him.

It took less than two minutes for Frankie's prized Rawlings mitt to be reduced to a pile of shredded, brown leather pieces.

Laura called her mother at work and begged her to come home right away. As she spoke, she could hear Frankie sobbing so hard, he could barely catch his breath.

"It's okay," they whispered to him, rocking Frankie back and forth *"Mom will be home soon. Mom will get you a new baseball glove. It's okay, Frankie, it's okay, it's okay. Everything is going to be okay."*

In Laura's apartment Maurice put the silver-framed photo back in its place on the dresser. Just as he did, he heard Laura yell out from the kitchen.

"Dinner's ready!"

She came out holding a big tray with a beautiful brown roasted chicken. Laura put it down on the dinner table.

"I set the table," Maurice told her. "But I don't know if I did it right. Maybe you can teach me?"

Laura didn't say anything. She just smiled and picked up one of the dinner plates and set it across from the other plate, on the other side of the table. Then she took one of the knives and one of the forks and put them on either side of the plate. She did the same with the other fork and knife. Finally, she folded the napkins in half and put one on the side of each plate. She did it all slowly so that Maurice could watch and understand for next time. It was just how she showed him how to use his steak knife at the Hard Rock Cafe—not by telling him, but simply by showing him.

Maurice watched as Laura used a carving knife to cut the chicken into beautiful slices. When she was done, she put three big pieces of chicken on Maurice's plate, followed by three big spoonfuls of mashed potatoes. It was, Maurice thought, a feast fit for a king. He picked up his fork and dug into the mashed potatoes and put a big portion into his mouth. They were delicious—*beyond* delicious. Then Maurice took his knife and cut through a piece of chicken just as he had cut through his steak at the

Hard Rock Cafe. It still wasn't easy to do, but the chicken was a lot softer than the steak, and Maurice was able to make his way through the first two pieces without too much trouble at all.

When Maurice was down to just a single piece of chicken left on his plate, he stopped eating.

"What's the matter?" Laura asked. "Aren't you hungry?"

"I'm okay," Maurice said.

"Don't you want your last bit of chicken?"

"I do," Maurice answered. "But . . . can I take it home with me?"

Maurice didn't want to tell Laura that he wanted to bring some chicken back home for his mother and sisters.

"Maurice, go ahead and eat it," Laura said. "You can eat all the chicken you want, then I'll wrap up whatever's left over so you can take some home, too, okay?"

"Okay," Maurice said, before digging into his last piece of chicken. When he was finished, Laura put two more pieces of chicken on his plate. Maurice enjoyed every last bite.

"Ready for dessert?" Laura asked.

"You bet," Maurice said.

He remembered Laura saying dessert was chocolate chip cookies, but he couldn't see cookies anywhere. Instead, Laura reached into the refrigerator and took out a thick tube of something.

"This is cookie dough," she explained. "We're going to pop this tube and make the cookies from the dough."

Laura banged the tube against the side of the kitchen counter, and, sure enough, the tube popped open. She peeled away the outer cardboard layer and was left with a roll of soft dough. Laura placed the dough in front of Maurice, and then put a large metal tray on the counter next to the dough. She took out a roll of tinfoil, ripped off a sheet, and put it on the tray.

"Okay, Maurice, would you like to cut through the dough and place each of the quarters onto the tray a few inches apart?" Laura said. "Then we'll put them in the oven and bake them. They should be in ready in about fifteen minutes."

Maurice didn't know there was a process for making cookies. He didn't get to eat cookies all that often—practically never—but to him, cookies were just cookies. He didn't know they came from dough that you had to cut up and put on a tray and bake in an oven. He never thought about how cookies became cookies. And for sure he'd never been asked to do all that stuff himself. Yet here was Laura, asking him to do just that.

Well, Maurice thought, if she trusted him to do it, he might as well give it a shot. He started cutting through the soft dough and putting the smaller pieces on the tray. When he was done, Laura took the tray and slid it inside the oven.

"Want some milk with your cookies?" Laura asked.

Maurice nodded his head, hard. Laura took a carton of milk out of the refrigerator and poured out two glasses. In a few minutes the smell of baking dough filled the air. It was another one of those overwhelmingly delicious smells. Maurice breathed in deep and imagined what the cookies would taste like.

"I like baking things," Laura said. "It's fun to follow the instructions, and do the work, and then sit back and wait for the goodies to bake. It's very . . . satisfying. Do the work, get the reward. Do you understand what I mean, Maurice?"

Maurice nodded yes. The way Laura was talking, it sounded kind of like a school lesson. And maybe, in a way, it *was* a lesson. About what, Maurice didn't yet know.

In another few minutes Maurice heard a bell ring over the oven.

Laura put on a big blue oven mitt and took out the tray, turning to show Maurice the cookies. They had grown from little slices of dough into big round circles, with little bits of chocolate shining through. Laura waited for the cookies to cool off, then put them on a plate and took them out to the dinner table. She and Maurice sat at the table dipping their cookies into their glasses of milk. The cookies were still hot, and they melted in Maurice's mouth. They were unlike anything Maurice had ever tasted.

He ate three big cookies before Laura was even finished with one.

Before long, there were only three chocolate chip cookies left on the plate. Laura took them into the kitchen and wrapped them in tinfoil. She put them in a paper bag, alongside another little packet of tinfoil, which was wrapped around three sizable pieces of chicken.

"These are for you to take home," Laura said.

Leftovers! Maurice had never had leftovers before.

Maurice thanked Laura for dinner, and she walked him to the elevator. She promised to see him the following Monday, at seven o'clock on the same corner, and she let him get in the elevator alone. Maurice rode it down to the lobby, holding tight to his bag of food. When the elevator opened in the lobby, Maurice saw Steve, the man in the suit and cap, talking to someone near the revolving door. Maurice ran through the lobby and pushed through the revolving door before Steve even had the chance to notice him.

Then Maurice ran back to the Bryant Hotel, and back to his family's apartment. He couldn't wait to see the look on his mother's face when he got home with all that chicken, but when he came through the door she wasn't home. But his sisters and Grandma Rose were. He showed them the chicken and the chocolate chip cookies, and was just as excited to see the look of surprise on their faces.

"Where'd you get these?" his sister Celeste asked him as she devoured one of the cookies.

"I just got 'em," Maurice answered. He didn't want to say any more, because he thought that if he told them the truth, they would laugh at him. Grandma Rose just stared at him.

Maurice stopped talking. He didn't tell them he baked the chocolate chip cookies himself, with a little help from a friend.

8

THE FOLLOWING MONDAY, MAURICE met Laura on Fifty-Sixth Street for their weekly get-together. This time Laura took him to the Broadway Diner on Fifty-Fifth Street. The Broadway Diner was another restaurant Maurice had passed at least a hundred times, but he'd never gone in. He'd even peered through the windows just to see what the people were eating. Yet it remained one of those places that were off limits to someone like Maurice.

With Laura, however, Maurice finally got to go inside.

It was a bright, shiny room with lots of neon lights and narrow tables. A woman near the front of the diner showed Laura and Maurice to their seats. The table had four chairs, even though there were only two of them. Maurice was happy to see that they would have the whole table to themselves. A waiter came by and handed Laura two enormous menus, and Laura gave one to Maurice.

The menu was even bigger than the one in the Hard Rock Cafe. Pages and pages filled with photos of the most delicious-looking platters—steak and potatoes, burgers and French fries, eggs and pancakes. Coming in, Maurice was sure he was going to order a big cheeseburger, but the photos of lots of different kinds of eggs looked too good to pass up. When Laura asked him what he was getting, he said, "Eggs."

"Eggs?" Laura said. "For dinner?"

Maurice wasn't sure what she meant. What was wrong with having eggs at night? Laura must have noticed Maurice's confused look, because she quickly told him that ordering eggs was perfectly okay.

"It's just that eggs are usually for breakfast," she said. "But you can have them if you want."

Maurice didn't understand why there were set times for meals—breakfast, lunch, dinner. In Maurice's world, everyone ate whenever there was food around. Didn't matter what time, or what food.

The waiter came back and smiled at Laura and Maurice.

Maurice noticed that even though he was still in the same dirty sweatpants and shirt, when he was with Laura, people treated him differently. They smiled at him instead of avoiding him. They paid attention to him instead of pretending he was invisible.

It felt good.

"Young man, what'll it be?" the waiter said.

"I'll have eggs," he said.

"All right, how do you want them?" the waiter asked.

Maurice wasn't sure how to answer the question, so he didn't say anything.

"Fried, scrambled, over easy?" the waiter asked.

Now Maurice was really confused. He wasn't sure what any of those terms meant. But he took a guess and went with the one that sounded the most fun. "Over easy. Please."

Maurice also ordered pancakes and a glass of orange juice. When the orange juice came, Maurice looked at it but didn't take a sip. He just sat there, afraid to take a sip.

"What's wrong?" Laura asked.

"Miss Laura, it looks really bad," Maurice told her. "There's all this stuff floating on top."

"That's just the pulp. It means the orange juice is really fresh. It was squeezed out of real oranges a few minutes ago. It's okay to drink it with pulp."

Pulp. One more thing Maurice had never heard of. But he trusted what Laura was telling him, so he took a sip and he was surprised that it tasted really tangy and really delicious. He took another sip, and another, and then he took one last big gulp and finished the whole glass.

Laura ordered him another glass of orange juice.

Halfway through the meal, Laura said, "You mentioned that you like watching baseball games, right? Have you ever been to a baseball game? I mean, in person?"

"Nah," Maurice replied. "Just watched 'em on TV."

"Well," Laura said, "how would you like to go to Shea Stadium and see the Mets play?"

Before Maurice could say anything, Laura took an envelope out of her purse, took out two tickets, and placed them on the table. Maurice stared at the tickets. He recognized the New York Mets logo on them—a stitched baseball with tall buildings and the word "Mets" inside it, in front of two crossed baseball bats. There were a few other words on the ticket he didn't understand, but he knew enough to know that the tickets meant he'd be able to go *inside* Shea Stadium in Queens and watch the Mets play baseball. *In person.* The thought of seeing a game that close up filled Maurice with a feeling of excitement that was completely new to him.

"I wanted to surprise you," Laura said. "My boss has season tickets to the Mets, and she gave me these when I told her how big of a Mets fan you are. What do you think? You want to go?"

"Yes!" Maurice practically yelled. "I really, really, really want to go!"

"Great!" Laura said, laughing. "The game is next Saturday, but before we can go, I need you to do something."

Uh-oh, Maurice thought. *Nothing for nothing.* Laura had promised Maurice that all she wanted from him was his friendship. But how could he be sure she meant it?

"What do you need me to do?" Maurice asked.

Laura took a folded sheet of paper out of her purse. Then she unfolded it and slid it over the table to Maurice.

"I need your mother's permission to be able to take you to the game," Laura said. "All it says is that your mother knows I am taking you to the game and she is okay with me driving you to the game in my car. You need to have your mother read

73

this whole page, then have her sign her name on the line at the bottom. Do you understand?"

"Yes, Miss Laura," Maurice said.

"Let's meet on Wednesday evening, and you can bring the signed paper with you," Laura said. "Then we'll go to the game on Saturday. Sound good?"

"Yes, Miss Laura," Maurice said again.

Some of the excitement Maurice had been feeling went away. In fact, *all* of it went away. Going to Shea Stadium to see the Mets play—*that* was exciting. Maurice couldn't even think of something he'd want to do more than that, except maybe go to Madison Square Garden to see his favorite professional wrestler, Hulk Hogan, get in the ring and throw some people around. Going to the baseball game wasn't the problem.

The problem was getting his mother to sign the paper.

His mother didn't even *know* about Laura. Only Grandma Rose did, and what he had shared with her wasn't very much. How was he going to, all of a sudden, show up with some paper from Laura for his mother to sign? How could he possibly explain it to her? *Some strange lady wants to take you to a Mets game?* she'd say. *Are you crazy? You know better than to trust a stranger.* Then she'd probably rip the paper into a hundred pieces.

When they finished their meal, Maurice took the piece of paper, said thank you and good night to Laura, and ran back to the Bryant. But before he went in, he took the paper and ripped it in half, and threw it in a garbage can.

That's what his mother was going to do anyway. Why not just do it himself?

On Wednesday night Maurice left his apartment to go meet Laura on Fifty-Sixth Street at seven. But at the last minute, instead of going to the corner where they always met, he ran across the street and hid behind a car where Laura couldn't see him. He didn't have the signed paper with him, and he knew Laura would be disappointed, and maybe she'd even be mad at him, so why bother? This was going to end eventually, might as well be today. Maurice decided he would stay across the street and wait for Laura to show up, then head home.

Sure enough, Laura arrived at the corner at exactly seven. Maurice could tell what time it was from a big clock in the window of a clothing store behind him. He watched as Laura stood on the corner and looked around. She turned right and left. She looked behind her and down the block. She walked back and forth, probably hoping to see Maurice running toward her from down the street, late as always. She waited and waited and waited. From the clock in the window, Maurice could see that Laura waited for him a whole half hour.

Finally, at seven thirty p.m., Laura left.

Suddenly, Maurice felt bad. He felt bad about letting Laura down. He felt bad for making her wait on the corner for half an hour. And he felt bad that he wasn't going to get to go to the Mets game on Saturday. Laura had told him they had great seats—way down in front, only a few rows away from the field. He would get to see all his favorite players up close—Mookie Wilson, Darryl Strawberry, Doc Gooden. He might even catch a foul ball! But that wasn't going to happen now. He thought about what his mother or his grandmother would say about it.

That's her world, they'd say. *That's not your world.*

And they were right.

Maurice slowly walked back to the Bryant. Suddenly, he realized that by not meeting Laura that evening, he also gave up the chance of having dinner. Now he wouldn't get to eat at all. As soon as he thought about that, he felt the familiar pain in his stomach, the dull ache, the heavy pull. He hadn't even realized how hungry he was, but now he did. And there was no dinner in sight.

Grandma Rose was in her chair, as always, and his mother and two of his uncles were just hanging out on the floor. They weren't sleeping, but Maurice could tell that they were already drifting away, disappearing into their distant worlds. He knew that when they disappeared like that, they wouldn't even know he was there, so he didn't bother saying hi or asking his mother if there was any food. Instead, he went straight inside his dark closet and closed the door behind him.

Maurice tried his best to fall asleep, but he couldn't. His stomach hurt too much. But he kept his eyes closed and kept trying. In a way, he was trying to disappear too. His mother could do it, and his uncles—they always drifted off with smiles on their faces, going to some happy place Maurice didn't understand. Maybe Maurice could do it too.

He thought about what his happy place would be, and he settled on Shea Stadium. As he lay in the darkness of the closet with his eyes closed, he tried to picture the stadium, with its bright green grass and its brown dirt infield. He tried to picture the players in their bright white uniforms—Mookie Wilson making a diving catch in the outfield. Doc Gooden striking out a player with his blistering fastball. Darryl Strawberry hitting another monster home run. Maurice tried to picture the baseball sailing through the bright blue sky, and finally landing in the outfield seats, and one lucky fan catching the ball and holding it up so everyone in the whole stadium could see that he'd caught it.

Maurice imagined that lucky fan was him.

Soon enough, Maurice started to fall asleep for real. But just as he was about to drift off, he heard a soft knock on the front door. He listened for a while, but nobody in the apartment moved to see who it was. Then there was another knock, louder this time. And another. Maurice opened the closet door just an inch to see if anyone was going to answer the knock.

Finally, he saw his mother slowly get up from the floor and make her way to the door. He watched as she walked slowly to the door, nearly tipping over, then straightening herself out. The knocking continued, and after what seemed like a long time, Maurice watched as his mother opened the front door.

"Hello," he heard someone say. "I'm looking for Maurice's mother."

The voice was familiar. Very familiar. Suddenly, Maurice realized who it was.

His heart started racing in fear.

It was Laura.

Through the door, he heard Laura say, "Thank you so much, and please tell Maurice to meet me on Saturday at eleven thirty at our usual place!"

That's when Maurice truly realized what it all meant.

He was going to a baseball game.

Maurice was extremely excited, but before he and Laura could go to the game, he knew there was one thing he had to do. On the day after Laura came to his room in the Bryant, Maurice ran up to the Symphony, and asked the doorman to tell Laura he was there. The doorman gave Maurice a funny look, but called up to Laura anyway. She told the doorman to send Maurice up.

"Miss Laura, you have to promise me that you'll never, ever go back to that place again," Maurice said as soon as Laura opened her apartment door. "Nice white ladies like you should never be in a place like that. You don't belong there. You must never go back. Promise me you'll never go back."

"It's okay, Maurice," Laura said. "I won't go back. I promise."

On Saturday, Maurice met Laura on the corner of Fifty-Sixth Street. They walked toward Broadway, to the garage where Laura kept her car. In the garage they walked over to a silver Chrysler LeBaron—Laura's car. Maurice didn't know anyone who owned a car, much less a car as nice as the LeBaron.

They pulled out of the garage and cruised toward the Queensboro Bridge, which would pass over the East River and take them to Flushing Meadow and Shea Stadium.

9

WHAT WAS SHE DOING here? Maurice thought. Why would she come to the Bryant? This wasn't a good place for her to be! It was too dangerous! Why would she come into his world?

Maurice kept the closet door open one inch so he could watch, but he kept quiet so no one would know he was there.

He looked on as his mother stood at the front door, wobbling from side to side, saying nothing. He looked at Laura, who was standing next to another woman, whom he later learned was her friend. The Bryant's security guard was standing beside them. Maurice could see Laura's face, and he could tell that she was confused. She must have been wondering if this woman in front of her was Maurice's mother. And if she was, Laura must have been wondering why she wasn't answering.

"I'm Laura," he heard her say. "I'm Maurice's friend. I'm sure he's mentioned me. Are you his mother?"

Darcella didn't answer. She just stood there, teetering.

"I want to take Maurice to a Mets game," Laura went on.

"Did he mention that to you? Anyway, I would like to have your permission to take Maurice to the game in my car. Can you sign this permission slip?" Still no answer. "I need his mother to sign it," Laura went on. "Is that you? Are you his mother?"

Maurice watched as his mother leaned against the door frame. Finally, she turned around and began stumbling back toward the rear of the room. Her eyes were open, but just barely, and Maurice knew she was already far, far gone. He hoped that Laura would just leave before anything bad happened, but instead she stayed, peering into the apartment. From the look on her face, Maurice could tell she was surprised by what she saw.

Of course she would be, considering how nice her own apartment was. She had a kitchen and a dinner table and a bureau and pictures on the wall and a fancy rug on the floor and a refrigerator full of food, and Maurice's apartment didn't have any of that. Maurice was embarrassed.

As Laura stayed in the doorway, Maurice saw Grandma Rose get up from her chair.

Oh no! Maurice thought. *This isn't good.*

Maurice could only imagine what Grandma Rose would have to say to Laura. Or maybe she wouldn't say anything at all, and instead just take a swing at her. For a second Maurice thought about racing out of the closet and trying to protect Laura from his grandmother, but he stayed where he was, watching silently, hoping for the best.

Grandma Rose went right up to the door and stopped just a foot or two away from Laura and her friend. Laura took a

small step backward. *Here it comes*, Maurice thought.

"You that white lady Maurice talked about," Rose said.

"Yes, that's me," Laura said, sounding relieved. Then she stuck out her hand, but Grandma Rose wasn't interested in any handshake.

"What you want?" she asked Laura.

"I want to take Maurice to a baseball game on Saturday," Laura said. "I don't know if he mentioned it. But I know he loves baseball and he's never been to a game, and I just thought . . . well, I thought it might be fun."

Grandma Rose silently stood her ground, staring at Laura in her frightening way.

"But before I can take him, I need his mother, or someone in his family, to sign this permission slip," Laura said. She held out the piece of paper in one hand, and a pen in the other, for Rose to take.

Maurice waited for the worst to happen. Maybe Rose would rip up the paper, maybe she'd push Laura into the hallway, or maybe she'd yell and holler at her and the security guard would have to step in. But, instead, the strangest, most unexpected thing happened.

Grandma Rose took the piece of paper, and then she took the pen. She signed the paper on the bottom line. Then she handed the paper and pen back to Laura, and slammed the front door in her face.

Wow. Maurice couldn't believe it. *How come Grandma didn't slug her?*

They got there in about a half an hour, and Laura parked in the enormous lot outside the stadium. Maurice looked up at Shea Stadium with awe as they walked toward Gate F. He had seen it on TV, and he understood it was a pretty big building, but he had no idea just *how* big. Up close, it was magnificent! It was round and it looked as if it kept going in each direction for miles. Meanwhile, hundreds of people poured out of the elevated subway cars and streamed through the lot toward the entrance gates, joining Maurice and all the people who had driven there.

They got to the entrance gate, and Laura handed the two shiny tickets to a ticket taker, who motioned for them to go on in. The feeling inside the stadium was electric, like everyone's excitement pooled together to form one big, tremendous feeling of happiness. Maurice couldn't control his excitement, and he found himself practically skipping through the concourse hall to their seats. Maurice believed he was too old to be skipping anywhere. But he just couldn't help it; he was that excited.

Not much later he and Laura turned left, out of the concourse and into a small tunnel that sloped upward and led to the playing field. Maurice held his breath yet again. As they walked up the tunnel, Maurice could see the wide-open sky in front of him. As he kept going, he saw a little piece of the outfield come into view. Then they were at the end of the tunnel, and the whole playing field opened up. Maurice's mouth dropped open.

It was the most glorious thing he'd ever seen.

LAURA SCHROFF

The impossibly green grass of the outfield stretched across most of the playing field, shimmering in the bright afternoon sun. A few players were already on the field, taking swings, playing catch, stretching, jogging. The tickets Laura had were for seats in the section that was closest to the playing field, only a few rows behind first base. That meant Maurice could clearly see the players on the field. He noticed his favorite player, Mookie Wilson, right away, and he felt a surge of joy. Could this be real? Was he actually just a hundred feet away from his hero? He was practically close enough to have a catch with him! When they finally got to their seats, Laura and Maurice sat down, but Maurice was too excited to sit still. He bounced up and down in his seat, staring out at the awesome field and listening to the sweet, crisp crack of the baseball bat in the fall air.

It felt like a little slice of heaven.

Soon, a man came around carrying a big square tub filled with hot dogs. Another man sold them soda, and another sold them two boxes of Cracker Jack. Maurice ate everything that came his way, but he only ate with one hand so he could keep his other hand free to try to catch any foul balls.

The game was incredible. When he watched the Mets on TV, Maurice was used to seeing tiny figures scamper around on a small, blurry, black-and-white screen. But now the game unfolded in front of him in the most spectacular way. Everything was bright and colorful and real. Maurice was close enough to hear the players shouting things at each other, and to hear the umpire yell, "Strike one!" He was close enough to hear the thump of a baseball settling into a baseball glove, and the brisk wallop of a ball jumping off a baseball bat. He could see the players running around the bases, so fast their batting helmets flew off. He caught the smiles on their faces when they hit home runs.

Maurice didn't catch a foul ball, but that was okay. The Mets won, beating the Philadelphia Phillies 6–4, and Mookie Wilson had two base hits. Maurice ate two hot dogs, a box of Cracker Jack, and a big fresh pretzel, and drank two Diet Cokes.

When the game ended, he and Laura filed out, joining the slow procession of thousands of other happy fans.

When they were back in the garage, Maurice thanked Laura for taking him to the game and buying him so many special things. Then he ran down Broadway, back toward the Bryant.

That night, in his closet, Maurice slept deeply and happily. He replayed the whole Mets game as he drifted off—every hit, every catch, every inning. But by the time he got to the middle of the first inning, he was fast asleep.

10

THE HUNGER STARTED BUILDING again the day after the baseball game. No matter how many hot dogs Maurice had eaten the day before, this was a new day, and the hunger started all over again, with a vengeance. It never went away for too long. It was always there, waiting to take over his life. Waiting to be the only thing that mattered.

Besides meeting Laura on Mondays, and begging for change to buy a slice of pizza or a Big Mac, there was one other way that Maurice sometimes found food. It wasn't something he liked to do, but if he absolutely had to, he would. When there were no other options, Maurice would go to the place he disliked the most, a place where he never felt welcome.

On those desperate days, Maurice would go to school.

Like his sisters, Maurice was enrolled in a public school in lower Manhattan. When he first began attending the school, he went to class five days a week. But before long some of the other students began making fun of him because of the way he dressed. His clothes were old and dirty, and sometimes he smelled bad, and the other kids would tease him about it and that would make Maurice mad. Sometimes it made him so mad that he would get into a fight with another student. His teacher, Miss House, would break up the fight and have Maurice sit in a special desk way in the back of the classroom, all by himself. Maurice didn't want to fight anyone, but sometimes his anger just took over. He didn't like anyone making fun of him or his tattered clothes. Instead of being kind to him, his classmates just poked fun at him. Life was hard enough without also being the butt of their jokes.

The only good thing about going to school was getting a free school lunch. Most of the students brought their own lunches in brown paper bags, but the students who didn't bring any food could get a free lunch. Sometimes it was only a sandwich, but on a good day, it was a hot meal. Often it was the only food Maurice would eat all day.

Still, Maurice didn't like going to school, and on most days he didn't. His teacher would urge him not to skip school so much, but for Maurice, it was easier to stay away. At school, there were rules and regulations and things you had to do, and if you didn't do them, you would be scolded or punished. Maurice didn't like being told what to do. On the streets there weren't any regulations. Maurice preferred the streets to the schoolroom. It was as simple as that.

Sometimes he would hear an adult say something like, "Oh, how terrible that this young child has to be out on the streets so much." Or, "If only this poor child could be in school instead of out on the street." But what they didn't understand was that, to Maurice, the streets *were* his school. The streets were where he learned things. On the streets he learned the most important lesson of all. It wasn't math or English or spelling.

It was how to survive.

And Maurice had been surviving on the streets ever since he was a little boy.

After Maurice's father, who was always called Junior, disappeared for good when Maurice was six, his immediate family shrank down to just four people: his mother, his two sisters, Celeste and LaToya, and Maurice. The four of them were an inseparable team—they went everywhere together, did everything together, survived together. At that point Maurice's mother, Darcella, was just beginning to give in to her sickness, but she wasn't nearly as bad as she would get when Maurice was older. Much of the time she was alert and engaged in what was happening around her. She had to be, because it was up to her to keep her young children safe and alive. No one else was there to help.

Back in those days the biggest challenge for Darcella was finding a place for her family to stay. She didn't have a job and she couldn't afford to rent a regular apartment, so she had to rely on shelters—places rented out by the city to provide temporary housing for families without homes. The shelters could be anywhere—in an old beat-up motel near LaGuardia Airport; in an unused gymnasium or armory; in an apartment building like the Bryant. What most of these shelters had in common was that you could only stay in them for a short period of time—maybe just a few weeks, and sometimes longer if you were lucky. Then you had to move on and find another place to live.

The first few times they were forced to move, Darcella took Maurice and his sisters to a friend's or a cousin's apartment, and they would sleep there for a few nights. But, inevitably, Darcella would get into an argument about something, or maybe even a fight, and she and the kids would get kicked out. Then it was on to the next apartment for a few nights. When the friends and cousins finally ran out, Darcella turned to the shelters, but sometimes she would get into fights with the people there, too, and they would be asked to leave.

Maurice remembered that sometimes his family would get kicked out in the middle of the night, even if it was freezing cold outside. He and his sisters would gather up their meager bundles of clothes and shuffle out onto the bitter streets. Darcella would lead them down dark alleyways and empty avenues, never telling them that she had no idea where they were going to sleep that night.

To make them feel less afraid, Darcella would often sing to them. She had a beautiful voice, full of soul and emotion; when she was younger, she sang in a church choir. Maurice *loved* hearing his mother sing. Sometimes she'd sing old gospel songs, but Maurice's favorites were when his mother made up songs right on the spot. She would point to something on the street—an abandoned car, a burned-out trash can, a stray cat—and work it into a lyric. And her songs would always end with the same lines:

> *How can this be*
> *Me and my three*
> *Living so desperately*

Maurice didn't understand what the words meant, but the sweet way his mother sang them made him feel safer and less afraid.

And just when Maurice believed he couldn't get any colder or sleepier, his mother would lead the three of them into the basement of a crummy old building, where other people were sleeping or talking or just lying around, and she would find an empty corner somewhere, and she would somehow scrounge up a blanket, and the children would curl up against one another under the blanket and try to sleep, while Darcella talked to the other people in the basement. About what, Maurice had no idea.

It was around then that his mother's sickness began to really take hold of her.

Maurice started to notice his mother sneaking off to the side, or hiding behind something, and disappearing for a minute or two. And when she'd come back, she would be different: less angry and twitchy and upset. Sometimes, when she was in this strange other place, Darcella would sing to her children some more, the same beautiful gospel songs, and then the singing would turn into humming, and then the humming would stop, and Darcella would fall fast asleep.

For Maurice, this was a good thing. He liked seeing his mother go to this strange distant place. In the beginning, Darcella's calm exterior wasn't a bad thing at all. It made her seem happy, if only for a short while.

Eventually, though, as Maurice got older, he realized his mother's sickness *wasn't* a good thing.

But even then, even when his mother's sickness got really bad, Maurice knew he could count on one thing.

He could count on the knowledge that his mother loved him.

Not once, not even for a single moment, did Maurice ever doubt that his mother loved him and wanted to give him the world, even if she wasn't always able to provide it. And he loved his mother dearly, and always would. He and his mother and his sisters were a team, forever—*me and my three*. That love, his family, were enough to keep Maurice going, even when things got really bad.

Other people didn't understand it. He knew they felt sorry for Maurice, because he spent so much time on the streets. He knew that people criticized his mother for not taking care of her children the right way, or not keeping their clothes clean, or not making sure they didn't go hungry. Maybe they even thought Darcella was a bad mother. But Maurice didn't think that way. He knew his mother was sick, but that never changed the love she felt for him and his sisters.

And love, Maurice understood, was more powerful than anything in the world.

During the days following the baseball game, Maurice didn't go to school at all. Even when he got painfully hungry, he didn't go. He just didn't want to deal with the other students making fun of his dirty sweatpants and sweatshirt this week. By the time the next Saturday rolled around, Maurice had managed to eat only one slice of pizza and some bread. He felt like he'd been punched in the gut. And yet, his Monday night dinner with Laura was still two whole days away. Maurice thought about all his options, and decided to do something he didn't really want to do.

He decided to go to the Symphony, to see if he could find Laura.

Maurice slowly entered the building's magnificent lobby and looked around for Steve. Sure enough, there he was, standing by the elevators. There was no way around it—to get to Laura, Maurice would have to talk to Steve again. He summoned up all his toughness and walked straight up to him. "I need to talk to Laura . . . please."

The doorman looked down at Maurice and seemed surprised. "What's your name again?"

"Maurice."

"Maurice, that's right," Steve said. "Don't I always see you walking around outside, begging for money?"

Maurice's instinct was to kick Steve in the knees and run

past him into the elevator, but instead he kept his cool.

"Can you tell Laura I'm here?" Maurice said.

For a moment Maurice was afraid the doorman would simply grab him by the collar and drag him out of the lobby. But then Maurice noticed Steve's face soften. He didn't look quite so angry anymore. Instead, he smiled and picked up the intercom telephone at the front desk.

"Sure, little buddy," he said.

Maurice rode up in the elevator and found Laura waiting for him just outside her door in the hallway.

"Maurice, are you okay?" she asked.

Maurice thought about how to answer the question, and realized there was only one way to do it—be honest.

"I'm sorry to bother you, but I'm really hungry, Miss Laura," he said.

"Let me get my jacket," Laura said. "Then we'll go to McDonald's."

At McDonald's, Maurice had his usual meal—Big Mac, French fries, chocolate milk shake. The food tasted even more delicious than all the other times he'd eaten there. Hunger could do that—it could make anything at all taste like the most delicious thing ever.

After the meal Laura looked at Maurice with a worried expression.

"Maurice, when was the last time you had anything to eat?" she asked.

"Thursday," Maurice replied.

That was nearly three days earlier.

Then Laura said, "Listen, Maurice, I wish I could be there for you every time you're hungry, but I can't. But I also don't want you to go without food on the nights I don't see you, and we can do one of two things."

Maurice sat up and listened closely.

"I can either give you some money for the week to buy food, though you'd have to be really, really careful about how you spent it so it didn't run out. Or, when we meet on Monday nights, we can go to the supermarket together and I can buy all the things you love to eat and I will make you lunch. I'll leave your lunch downstairs with Steve, or at the front desk, and you can swing by and pick it up on the way to school."

Maurice thought about the two options—money or homemade lunch. They were both incredible, miraculous options, because they both meant he wouldn't have to go hungry in between Mondays. Ordinarily, the idea of being handed some money so he could buy food would be the very best option he could possibly imagine, but something Laura said made Maurice think a little longer about the other option.

She would make his lunch.

"If you make my lunch," Maurice finally asked Laura, "will you put it in a brown paper bag?"

Laura looked confused.

"Do you want your lunch in a brown paper bag? Or would you prefer it some other way?"

"Miss Laura, I don't want your money," Maurice said. "I just want lunch in a brown paper bag."

"Sure," Laura said. "But why is the paper bag so important?"

"Because when I see kids come to school with their lunches in a brown paper bag," Maurice said, "that means someone cares about them."

And so that's what happened. On Monday nights Laura would take Maurice to the supermarket on Eighth Avenue and buy all the things he loved to eat. They would pick out chicken and turkey and roast beef and cheese and whatever kind of sliced bread Maurice liked, a piece of fruit, a juice, and even some cookies or brownies for dessert. Then Laura would make lunch for Maurice and leave it with a doorman or at the front desk in the morning.

Maurice would swing by and pick it up, and he would proudly take his lunch in a brown paper bag to school.

He started going to school a lot more often.

In fact, all of a sudden, Maurice *wanted* to go to school.

He wanted the other kids to see him walk in with a brown paper bag, just like they did.

11

MAURICE WAS SPENDING MORE and more time at school. He didn't go every day; in fact, some weeks, he went only one or two days. But some weeks he went three or four days in a row. The old problems were still there—his dirty clothes, the way kids picked on him, how angry he got when anyone made fun of him—but, for some reason, Maurice felt better about going. He didn't feel the need to always get in fights with the other students, and he didn't feel quite as angry and frustrated as he used to—or at least he didn't feel that way *all* the time. He knew this was because he now wasn't hungry all the time.

During one of his Monday night dinners with Laura, Maurice said, "Miss Laura, can I ask you something?"

"Of course."

"My school is having a parent-teacher night," Maurice said, "and I was wondering if you could come."

Laura seemed surprised by the request, which Maurice kind of expected. After all, she was not his parent. She wasn't even related to him. He had a mother, and if anyone should attend his parent-teacher night at school, it should be her. But Maurice also knew that his mother wasn't going to be able to go.

In fact, the last time Maurice's mother, Darcella, had come to Maurice's school, it had not gone well. Maurice remembered the events of that day. He was enrolled as a special education student, which meant he had what the school called "developmental and/or social issues." In Maurice's case, the school considered him disadvantaged because of his difficulty picking up on things as quickly as the other students, due to the challenges of his home life. For Maurice, it was even simpler than that.

The reason he had so much trouble learning things at school was because he was always hungry. It's hard to pay attention to anything if all you can think about is how much your stomach hurts from being so empty.

Maurice's enrollment at the school required that one of his parents come in and speak with school officials during the school year, so the officials could check in on how things were going at home. Maurice was in school the day his mother showed up for her interview.

Maurice didn't see what happened. But later on he heard about it from some other students. As soon as Darcella sat down with the school principal for her interview, an argument started. What it was about, no one knew. But Darcella was angry—very angry—and there was a lot of yelling and screaming and pointing fingers. It was so loud that anyone outside the principal's office could hear it. Before long, another teacher asked Maurice's teacher, Miss House, to come down while she watched her class.

Maurice knew the commotion had to do with his mother. When school was over, he went up to Miss House to make sure everything was okay.

"Everything's going to be fine, Maurice," Miss House assured him. "Your mother is so proud of you. She knows how very bright and special you are."

After that, his mother never set foot in the school again.

"Maurice," Laura said, "what about your mother? Shouldn't she go with you?"

"Nah," Maurice said, "she's not gonna go."

"Maurice, I would be happy to go with you, but you need to tell your mother about it first and ask her if she can go. If she can't, then I'll go."

Maurice agreed to the deal. But when he got back to the Bryant that night, he didn't do what Laura had asked.

The next time he saw Laura, he told her again that his mother "wasn't gonna go." It wasn't a lie. But it wasn't the whole truth, either. Maurice didn't like not being entirely truthful, but sometimes he believed he had no other choice. There were things about his family, his life, his world, that Laura simply would not understand.

When Laura agreed to go to the school event with Maurice, he asked her another question.

"Miss Laura, when you come to the school, will you be wearing your same work clothes?"

Maurice was referring to the skirts and blouses and dresses and jackets he usually saw Laura wear.

"I don't know. I guess I could go home and change," Laura told him.

"No!" Maurice said. "Don't change. I want you to come in your work clothes."

"Why?" Laura asked.

"'Cause you always look so classy."

That week Maurice and Laura had their usual Monday night dinner. Then, two days later, Maurice met Laura at her garage around the corner from Broadway. She drove up the garage ramp in her silver LeBaron, and Maurice hopped in. Together they drove to his school.

Maurice eagerly watched and listened as Laura introduced herself to Miss House.

"Hi, I'm Laura Schroff. I'm so pleased to meet you."

"It's very nice to meet you, too," Miss House said warmly, shaking Laura's hand. "Maurice says so many nice things about you."

It was true. More and more, Maurice found himself telling Miss House about something he and Laura did together. Or he would say, "Miss Laura says this . . . ," or, "Miss Laura says that. . . ." Her name kept popping up. That's why Miss House didn't seem at all surprised to see Laura show up at the parent-teacher meeting instead of Maurice's mother.

"Maurice, do you mind stepping outside the classroom for a minute," Miss House asked. "I'd like to speak with Ms. Schroff privately."

Maurice felt a surge of dread. Why did Miss House want to speak with Laura privately? Was she going to tell her about all the fights Maurice got into? Or what a bad student he was? Was she going to say that being around Maurice so much wasn't safe for Laura?

Was she going to scare Laura enough that she might disappear?

Maurice didn't want to leave the classroom, but he did as he was told.

Instead of walking away down the hall, though, he stood just outside the classroom door, which allowed him to hear most of their conversation.

"You should know that Maurice is very proud of you," Miss House said to Laura. "He speaks about you often."

"Well, I'm very, very proud of Maurice, too," Laura said. "He's such a special boy."

"How in the world did you two meet?"

Maurice listened as Laura described their meeting on the corner of Fifty-Sixth Street, and the first of their many meals together.

"I hope I can make even a little bit of difference in his life," Laura said.

"You are," Miss House replied. "I worry about Maurice. He's always late to class, if he decides to show up at all. He's always getting into fights. He shows enormous anger at times. But he can also be very sweet and thoughtful, and he's obviously very smart. Since you came into his life, he's been coming to school a lot more often, and he's been getting into fewer fights."

"Well, that's good," Laura said.

"Ms. Schroff, I have to say something to you, and I'm going to be blunt," Miss House said.

Outside the classroom, Maurice braced himself. This was it, he thought. Miss House was about to ruin his friendship with Laura.

"Children like Maurice are always disappointed," Miss House continued. "Every day someone else lets them down. I hope you realize that you can't just come in and out of Maurice's life. If you are going to be there for him, you have to really be there for him. You can't just wake up one day and abandon this boy."

After a pause, Laura said, "I've only known Maurice for a few months now, but I already know that he is someone who is going to be in my life for a long, long time. I consider Maurice to be my friend. And I would never, ever walk out on a friend."

After the parent teacher conference, Laura asked Maurice where he wanted to have dinner.

"Can we go to Junior's in Brooklyn?" Maurice blurted out. "They are famous for the best cheesecake in the world! Can we please go?"

"Sure, why not?" she said.

During their dinner at Junior's—Maurice had a burger and fries, and, yes, a slice of the best cheesecake in the world for dessert—Laura told Maurice about her talk with Miss House.

"She cares about you a lot and she really wants you to do well in school," Laura said. "She says that you're very, very smart, and she is on your side."

Maurice felt a big smile spread across his face. When he overheard Miss House telling Laura that he was smart, he felt something he'd never felt before. Only later would he learn the word for it—pride. This was the first time he was experiencing a sense of accomplishment, of satisfaction about himself. And then, at Junior's, when he heard Laura repeat it, Maurice felt that pride burst through him all over again; he couldn't help but smile. It felt good to hear someone say he was smart. No, not just good—it felt *great*.

"But here's what she needs you to do, Maurice," Laura went on. "She needs for you to stop getting into fights, and to do your homework, and also—and this is important—she needs you to show up to class on time. Maurice, she says you are always, *always* late for class."

Maurice knew what the word "late" meant, and he certainly knew what the word "class" meant. But the idea that he was always late for class, he didn't quite understand. On the days he went to school, he got up in the morning and went to class right after getting up. What else was he supposed to do?

"Now, Maurice, I understand that with everything that's going on in your life, it can sometimes be hard to concentrate on your homework," Laura said. "But you have to try to find a way to get your homework done, if you possibly can. If your first class starts at seven thirty in the morning, you *have* to be there at seven thirty. You can even get there at seven fifteen just to be sure you're not late. You can't just show up at eight or eight thirty or whenever, Maurice. That is unacceptable. Do you understand?"

Something about Laura's firm tone of voice made Maurice put down his fork and stop eating his cheesecake. It also made the smile on his face go away. Worst of all, Laura's words made him want to cry. He didn't know why, they just did. And before he knew it, he *was* crying. Right there at his table in the middle of Junior's.

"Maurice, what's the matter?" Laura said. "Are you okay?"

"Miss Laura, you just don't understand," Maurice said. "There's no clock in my apartment at the Bryant. There are no watches, either. Miss Laura, I never know what time it is."

It was then Maurice realized why he'd started crying: Laura's firm tone made him feel like he had *disappointed* her. And that made him feel terrible.

"Maurice, it's okay. I'm sorry I was so hard on you," Laura said. "I didn't realize that was the problem. Don't worry, we can figure this out together. What if I get you an alarm clock?"

"I guess that would help," Maurice said.

"Tell you what," Laura said. "I'll get you an alarm clock that wakes you up on time, but I will also get you a watch so you always know what time it is. In return, you have to promise that you will do your best to try get to class on time every day. Can you promise me that?"

"Okay, I promise," Maurice said.

"Maurice, I know it's not easy," Laura said. "I know your life isn't easy. I just want you to know how proud I am of you for doing your best."

Maurice felt himself start to smile again. He liked hearing that Laura was proud of him, and it made Maurice feel like he could trust her a little more, and he decided to share something about himself with her.

"Miss Laura, for a long time I didn't believe that I could read or write," he told her. He explained how school officials had tested him, and afterward had informed his mother that he couldn't read and write. But Maurice knew that this wasn't true.

"I *knew* I could do it," he said. "It's just that I needed to do it very slowly, probably slower than other kids my age. But after a while I just started believing what everyone was saying about me, and once I started believing that, doing good at school wasn't important anymore."

Laura listened closely as Maurice spoke. Finally, she said something.

"Maurice, did I ever tell you that I was a *terrible* student?" she said.

Maurice could hardly believe what she was saying. How could Laura have possibly been a bad student? She was so successful!

AN INVISIBLE THREAD

"It's true," Laura said. "I was an awful student. I flunked a few classes in high school, and I never even went to college."

Maurice was truly surprised. It just didn't make any sense. How could Laura have done so well if she'd been so bad at school?

"Why were you a bad student?" Maurice finally asked.

"Let me tell you a story about my father," Laura said.

12

Nunziato's parents immigrated to America from Italy. Nunzie's father tried to teach his son many things, but perhaps the most important lesson was the value of hard work. And so Nunzie became an incredibly hard worker. He was twelve when he had his first job, shining shoes, and after that he never stopped working. He met Laura's mother, Marie, when they were both guests at a friend's wedding. Not much later they got married, and they went on to have five children.

Laura was their second child.

During Laura's childhood, her father built homes around Long Island during the day and worked as a bartender at night. Most of the time, Laura knew her father to be a sweet, funny, friendly man. Nunzie got along with everyone, and he had a way of making even strangers feel welcome. People would always come up to Laura and say, "I wish my father was more like yours."

But Laura knew something these people didn't know. She knew her father wasn't always the man everyone adored.

Nunzie would often transform into a different person. He would *become less sweet and funny. Sometimes he could get really mean and even frightening. Like the time he cut up poor Frankie's baseball mitt. There wasn't anything Laura or any of the children could do to stop their father from slipping into his terrible moods, and not even Laura's mother, Marie, could do anything to stop them.*

Instead, the family tried their best to find a way to live with them.

Sometimes Nunzie would come home after a long night's work, and his sickness would take hold of him. He would come through the door in the middle of the night and start yelling at Laura's mother or at one of their children—usually Frankie—for no good reason at all.

Everyone in the family woke up from the screaming. The children would stay in their beds, shaking with fear. After his tirade, Nunzie would finally fall asleep—but for everyone else, falling back asleep was hard. On Sundays, Nunzie worked during the day. But back in his home, as it got closer to six p.m., the time he usually got off work, his family would feel the terrible tension of not knowing what kind of mood Nunzie would be in when he finally arrived.

Sometimes the waiting and the fear and apprehension and tension were even worse than whatever Nunzie did.

Other times Nunzie's moods would lead to bad events.

Like the time Nunzie came home from work one Sunday night with a package of Flying Saucer ice-cream sandwiches from Carvel. Laura and her siblings loved Flying Saucers. The kids all came running over to eat them, and young Laura—who was just seven years old—got so excited, she couldn't help blurting, "I love these so much I could eat all of them by myself!"

Suddenly, Nunzie's face changed from happy to angry.

"Good," Nunzie said. "Now you're going to sit there and you're not going to get up until you eat every last one of those Flying Saucers by yourself."

The other children knew from their father's tone of voice that his mood had changed, so they jumped out of their chairs and ran out of the kitchen. That left Laura at the table by herself. She hadn't meant anything by her comment; she was just so excited to get an unexpected ice-cream treat. Certainly she hadn't been serious about wanting to eat the whole package—after all, there were six Flying Saucers in the package.

Nunzie glared at Laura and said, "Start eating."

If Laura's mother had been home, she would have stopped Nunzie from making Laura eat all the ice cream. Unfortunately, Marie was away (like Nunzie, she was an incredibly hard worker, and she was busy working at the catering hall that evening). Laura had no choice but to bite into the first Flying Saucer and not stop until it was finished. It was delicious, as she'd expected it to be, and when she was done she ate a second Flying Saucer pretty quickly too. But by the time she finished that one, she felt full. And there were still four more to go.

Nunzie sat at the kitchen table, watching Laura eat. And so Laura kept eating. She ate a third Flying Saucer, and a fourth. Somewhere around the fifth, Laura threw up and started to cry. Only then did Nunzie take the package and throw it in the sink, where the rest soon melted. That night she stayed awake, clutching her stomach. Then she cried herself to sleep.

Why had Laura's own father been so mean to her? There was no answer, other than the usual answer—it was part of his sickness.

And the way to deal with Nunzie's sickness was by pretending it didn't exist at all.

As Maurice listened to Laura's story, part of him felt sorry for her. But another part was surprised. Maurice was surprised that Laura's story about her childhood was a story that he could easily understand and identify with. In many ways, it wasn't very different from the story of his *own* childhood. For Maurice, it came as a shock that someone as successful and classy as Laura—someone who seemed so in charge of her life—could have gone through anything that was even a little similar to what he was going through.

After all, Maurice had grown up believing that there was *us*, and there was *them*.

Yet here was Laura, sharing a story that Maurice could not only understand but *relate* to. Maybe the distance between *us* and *them* wasn't quite as enormous as Maurice had thought.

"My point," said Laura, "is that with all the fighting that happened in our family, there were a lot of nights where I just couldn't fall asleep at all. And in the morning I would get up and I would be so groggy and so sleepy, and yet I had to go to school, same as every other kid who had probably had a great night's sleep. It was hard for me to be a good student when it took all my energy not to fall asleep at my desk, let alone concentrate on what was happening in class."

Maurice could understand that, too. For him, it was hunger. For Laura, it had been sleep.

"Now, I'm not making excuses for being a bad student. I'm

just saying that that's the way things were. And, unfortunately, I never really became a good student. I struggled through school and I decided not to go to college at all. I decided I was done with school, and I wanted to go straight into the working world. That was my plan."

"Then how did you get to be where you are now?" Maurice asked.

"Well," Laura said, "in high school I took a typing course so I could become a secretary. Then I saw an ad in a newspaper for a secretary's job, and I applied. It wasn't my dream job, but I knew I needed work experience, so I took it. Four months later I met a girl who worked for Icelandic Airlines, and she told me there was an opening for a secretary in her company. Their office was in Manhattan, and it was my dream to work in Manhattan, so I applied for the job and got an interview. I was determined to get that job."

"Then what happened?" Maurice asked.

"The next morning I went in for my interview and I sat down and took my typing test," Laura said. "And you know what happened?"

"No, what?"

"I failed," Laura said. "I was so embarrassed and so upset. I went up to the person who was supervising the test, and I said, 'Please, I was so nervous, and I didn't do anywhere near my best. Can you please let me take the test again?' And the lady must have felt sorry for me, because she let me retake the test. I sat down and started typing as fast as I could."

"And?" Maurice asked.

"I failed again," Laura said. "I failed even worse than the first time."

Maurice didn't understand. If Laura kept failing her test, how did that lead to her becoming so successful?

"Now the lady who was in charge of the test felt *really* sorry for me, so she let me sit down next to her so we could talk a little," Laura explained. "And as we talked, she got the chance to see me as a real person, not just some name on a list. I had the opportunity to tell her how determined I was, and how I would go back and practice my typing for a *thousand* hours if that's what it would take for me to pass the test and get the job. I made her understand that despite all the challenges I had faced, I was not going to let anything stop me from being successful."

"Then what?" Maurice asked.

"The woman saw something that made her believe in me, and she recommended me for a job as a receptionist. That way I didn't have to type a lot. But once I had my foot in the door, I never looked back. From that moment on I worked as hard as I could to prove to myself and to convince everyone else that I was a good worker. No, that I was a *great* worker. And that, Maurice, is how I got to where I am today."

Maurice sat there silently and tried to take it all in. Laura had failed both her typing tests, yet somehow she'd walked away with a job. In other words, she hadn't allowed someone else's judgment of her to be the final word.

It was a little like Maurice constantly being told that he couldn't read or write, when deep down inside he knew he *could* read and write. Maybe Laura was saying that she never allowed someone else's opinion to slow her down or force her to give up. All she needed in order to get the job and change the direction of her life was having one person—just *one* person—see something in her that made them believe she could do it.

And as he realized all these things, Maurice suddenly understood why Laura had chosen to share that story with him as they ate their slices of cheesecake.

It was her way of telling Maurice that *she* believed in *him*.

The following Monday, when Laura and Maurice met on the corner of Fifty-Sixth Street, Laura took him to a store on Broadway to pick out a new watch. Maurice picked out a white watch with blue numbers on the face. The watch also had an alarm-clock feature. Maurice told Laura it was the perfect watch for him—but that wasn't the real reason he chose it. He chose it because it had a long white strap that he could slip over his head. That way, he could always keep the watch with him, even while he slept. He would never have to worry about someone stealing it.

Laura showed Maurice how to set the alarm, and he set it for six forty-five a.m., so he could get up in time to get to school by seven thirty. The next morning Maurice got to school five minutes before his first class began.

13

ON ONE OF THEIR usual Monday dinners, Laura had a surprise for Maurice. She asked if he would like to come with her to visit her sister's house on Long Island. Maurice had no idea what or where Long Island was, but the thought of going on a trip was exciting. Especially a trip that would take him out of the city.

In fact, Maurice had never left the confines of the New York City area in his young life. All he knew was busy streets and concrete sidewalks and tall buildings. But as Laura explained it, the town where her sister Annette lived—a place called Greenlawn— was full of trees and fields and big backyards. Maurice didn't know what a backyard looked like either. Not one of the twenty places he'd lived in had had any kind of yard at all.

"My sister and her family can't wait to meet you, Maurice," Laura told him. "They're looking forward to your visit."

On Saturday morning Maurice and Laura drove along the Long Island Expressway for the one-hour trip to Annette's house.

Maurice was wearing a new pair of pants and a new blue sweat-shirt that Laura had bought for him. In the time they'd been together, Laura had bought quite a few things for Maurice—his own toothbrush, new sneakers, the watch with the alarm, and some other new clothes. Laura's friend Lou, who worked with her at *USA Today*, also gave Laura a huge bag of clothes for Maurice, and some of the shirts and pants still had their sales tags on them, which meant they were brand new. Maurice finally had some nice clothes to wear, and wearing them made him feel good about himself. Laura also bought him a small trunk with a lock on it, so no one could steal his clothes.

Still, he was nervous as he headed to Annette's house. He wondered if everyone there would be as nice to him as Laura was.

Laura pulled into the driveway of a big house on the corner of a tree-lined street. The house was a two-story Colonial with a big, rolling front lawn. When Maurice saw the house, and saw how big it was, he couldn't believe it was just for one family. It looked big enough for *ten* families to live in. Stepping out of Laura's car and onto the front lawn, Maurice felt as if he was stepping into a brand-new world.

When Laura and Maurice got to the front door, it was already open—and Annette and her family were waiting for them. So was Laura's other sister, Nancy. Laura introduced Maurice to Annette, and to Annette's husband, Bruce. Then Laura introduced him to the three young children standing alongside Bruce and Annette: Brooke, who was seven, Derek, who was nine, and Colette, who was about the same age as

Maurice—eleven. The children looked at Maurice in the way they would look at any new person showing up at their house— with curiosity. Maurice stared back at them in the same way.

"Come on, wanna see my room?" Derek asked Maurice, and without waiting for answer, he ran into the house toward the stairs. Maurice ran after him, and soon all the kids were upstairs showing Maurice their bedrooms. As he walked through them, Maurice was quiet. He was trying to take in everything he was seeing, because he'd never seen anything like it.

The children's bedrooms were beyond anything he could have ever imagined. Derek's room was full of baseball stuff and posters and toys and clothes, and the girls' bedrooms had lots of cute stuffed animals and frilly curtains and things like that. And their beds! The beds were fitted with colorful sheets and blankets and comforters, and they looked so incredibly comfortable! One of the beds even had several pillows on it. At the Bryant, there wasn't a single pillow in Maurice's apartment.

Maurice understood that other children in other situations lived differently than he did, and that many of them had more possessions and more clothes and more everything than he did. But it wasn't until he saw Derek's, Colette's, and Brooke's bedrooms that Maurice truly understood how much "more" they had than him.

"Come on, let's go play on the swings," Derek said, before dashing back downstairs. Maurice ran after him, and followed him into the big backyard that was enclosed by a long fence. There was a swing set, and a slide, and bars for climbing, and lots and lots of room to run around. If you tripped and fell, you fell on the perfect, soft grass, so you wouldn't get hurt anyway. It was like the best playground Maurice could have dreamed up in his head, and it was all for Derek and his sisters to play in! And now, on this remarkable Saturday, it was for Maurice to play in too.

After a while Derek yelled out, "Hey, let's go ride bikes!" and before Maurice knew it, he was in the big garage on the side of the house with Derek and Derek's father, Bruce. Bruce pulled out one bicycle for Derek, and another one for Maurice.

The two boys went out on the quiet street, and Derek pushed off and pedaled his bike quickly down the road. Maurice hesitated. He didn't hesitate because he didn't know how to ride a bike—he did. He'd ridden a bike before, outside one of the welfare shelters where he'd stayed.

He hesitated because he was amazed by how *easy* it all was.

In this world, if you wanted to ride a bike, you just went out and rode a bike. Your bicycle was safely tucked away in your garage, ready to go. And the street outside was big and wide and smooth, and maybe a single car drove down every few minutes, so it was a very safe place to ride. Just plain fun. The ease of it all filled Maurice with a kind of wonder, and that wonder was a good feeling—a really good feeling. It was a feeling he wished he could have all the time.

Only much later did Maurice realize what it actually was. *Freedom.* The kind that comes with being a kid.

Or at least a kid in the world where Derek lived.

Maurice spent the entire afternoon playing with Derek and his sisters. Not once did they ask him anything about his life, or where he lived, or why he was different from them, or anything like that. They all just played, and they were nice to him, and laughed with him, and had fun. Maurice realized that to Colette, Derek, and Brooke, he wasn't invisible, like he was to people on the streets.

To them, he was just another kid.

The rest of the day was one surprise after another. A room just for watching TV? A washer and dryer just for them? A bathroom downstairs and two more upstairs? Maybe the most surprising thing of all was that Annette had a special room that was used just for eating. Laura called it a "dining room." Maurice could hardly believe that people had special rooms just to eat food. In his world, people ate wherever and whenever they got food in their hands.

After more than two hours of swinging and bike riding and playing games, Maurice and the other kids were called into the dining room. By then, Maurice had already begun to smell the delicious aroma of food cooking. He followed Derek into the dining room, where he saw Laura waiting for him. She called him over and pointed to a seat beside her.

"You can sit next to me, okay?" she said.

After everyone was seated, Annette brought out large plates of food—a big roasted chicken, a big round bowl of mashed potatoes, another big bowl of broccoli, a basket filled with bread. It seemed like an endless procession of beautiful, appetizing dishes. All Maurice wanted to do was reach out and start eating, but by then he already knew that there was something he had to do first.

His napkin.

During one of their dinners together, Laura had taught Maurice how to take his napkin, unfold it, and place it on his lap before a meal. Maurice didn't quite understand why that was necessary, but as Laura explained it, putting your napkin on your lap before you ate was "good manners." So at Annette's dinner table, Maurice took the neatly folded cloth napkin off his plate, unfolded it, and laid it across his lap. Then he looked up at Laura.

She smiled and nodded.

Laura helped Annette put food on everyone's plate, and she made sure to load up Maurice's dish with everything. Maurice picked up his fork and knife and used them just how Laura had taught him. Once in a while Maurice would sneak quick looks at Laura, as if to ask, "Am I doing it right?" And Laura would smile, letting him know he was doing just great.

This time, instead of plowing through his food, Maurice tried to eat slowly. All the other children finished their dinners long before he did. Maurice was hungry, and he could have eaten just as quickly, but he didn't want to. He was having fun sitting at the big table with everyone else. Maurice wanted the meal to last as long as possible.

Then Maurice noticed something unusual.

Even when everyone was finished eating, they didn't get

up from the dinner table. Instead, they stayed in their seats and kept talking and laughing and telling jokes. Even after *dessert* was done, they all stayed in their seats. This was something Maurice didn't understand. Once you were done eating, why stick around? Yet here everyone was, hanging out at the table just to be with one another. It wasn't anything Maurice had ever seen happen.

When everyone finally did get up, Maurice checked the watch around his neck and realized the dinner had lasted nearly *two hours*. The average length of one of Maurice's meals was around five minutes.

After dinner Maurice followed Derek and his sisters into the room that was dedicated to watching TV. They all found comfortable spots on the big plush sofa and settled in to watch cartoons. Every once in a while Maurice would notice Laura peeking her head into the room, and he guessed she was checking to make sure he was okay.

"Laura, relax," he overheard Annette tell her. "He's doing fine."

Finally, it was time to go. The children all lined up to say good-bye to Maurice, and Annette and Bruce both gave him a big hug. Maurice thanked them for dinner, and for inviting him to their home. They asked him to come back soon.

Once in the car, Maurice was so tired from playing and so full from eating that he leaned his head against the window and fell asleep.

When he woke up, they were about twenty minutes away from New York City.

"Did you have a good time today?" Laura asked him.

"Miss Laura, I had the best time," Maurice said.

"So tell me, what was your favorite part of the day?"

Maurice didn't have to think about the question too long. He already knew what his favorite part was. And it wasn't the backyard, or the bike riding, or the TV room, or all the toys and games, or anything like that.

"My favorite part," Maurice said, "was the big table."

"The big table?" Laura said. "You mean the dining room table?"

"Yeah," Maurice said. "The food was great and all, but what I really liked was that everyone just sat around the table and talked."

Laura seemed surprised by his answer. Maybe she didn't fully realize how special sitting around that table had been to Maurice.

Because the table wasn't just a place where food got passed around.

No. It was a place where *love* went back and forth.

"Miss Laura," Maurice said, "someday, when I grow up, I'm gonna have a big table like that for me and my family. And we're all gonna sit around and talk and laugh just like your sister's family does."

Laura smiled. For a second it looked like she might even cry.

Just then Maurice realized that this was the first time he'd ever said anything to anyone about his future.

He'd never mentioned it before because he never thought

about it. His future simply meant figuring out where his next meal would come from or how to stay out of trouble. Maurice didn't dream of becoming a doctor or a fireman or an astronaut like a lot of other children, because he didn't know these were things he *could* dream of becoming. And, besides, what was the point of dreaming about something that was never going to happen?

And yet, right there in the car on the way home from Long Island, Maurice not only dreamed about his future, he shared the first dream he'd ever had about his future with Laura. It was clear and sharp and focused. It was to have a big table, and a big family, all his own.

"Well, Maurice," Laura said, "I have no doubt you will get that big table someday. I am sure of it."

Maurice looked back out the car window. The trees and front yards were gone now, replaced by sidewalks and buildings. The only traces of Maurice's wonderful day were the happy memories swirling around in his head, and a big bag of leftovers that Annette gave Maurice to share with his family.

And later that night, when Maurice finally went into his closet, it was those sweet memories that ushered him gently to sleep.

14

NOTHING MUCH HAD CHANGED with Maurice's family in the months since he'd met Laura. The good news was that they hadn't been kicked out of the Bryant Hotel, so they still had a roof over their heads. The bad news was that Maurice's mother, Darcella, was still in the grips of her sickness. She never seemed to get better, only worse. Sometimes she would now disappear for three or four days in a row, then reappear without any explanation. The only constants were Maurice's two sisters and Grandma Rose.

Maurice still didn't talk about Laura. Maurice had overheard Grandma Rose tell his mother, Darcella, about her once, but no one seemed too interested in the role Laura was playing in Maurice's life, so he decided not to bring her up.

Surely his mother had noticed some of the new things Maurice brought into the Bryant—new clothes, new toothbrush, things like that. But she never mentioned them or asked him about them. And that was fine with Maurice.

And while he always made a point of bringing food home for his sisters and for Grandma Rose, he didn't really want to share Laura with anyone in his family beyond that. She was his friend, and Maurice wanted to keep their friendship just the way it was.

So when Laura invited Maurice to spend Thanksgiving with her and her family, Maurice didn't bother to tell anyone in his family about it.

It wasn't like his family celebrated Thanksgiving, anyway. Maurice could remember only one or two times that his family had "celebrated" a holiday or a birthday or any other special day. They simply didn't have the luxury of treating any single day as more special than any other day. The struggles they all faced didn't go away just because the calendar said it was Thanksgiving or Christmas. In Maurice's world, every day was a battle to survive, and there was no such thing as a holiday from that battle.

Maurice knew what Thanksgiving was all about. And he knew the history behind the holiday, but he wasn't aware of the traditions that went into making it a special day. The only thing he knew for sure was that on Thanksgiving in New York City, something remarkable happened.

Thanksgiving was when the streets of Midtown would shut down, and the incredible Macy's balloons would parade down Broadway.

Maurice loved watching the giant helium-filled balloons floating past the massive crowds of people gathered on the sidewalks. Seeing the big, colorful cartoon floats of Snoopy, and Popeye the Sailor, and Kermit the Frog, and of course Superman, soaring sideways, arms extended, through the air, was unbelievable. But Maurice never felt like he was part of any "celebration."

Then came another of Laura's surprises.

She told Maurice that instead of going to her sister Annette's house for Thanksgiving, as she ordinarily would, this year the family would all come to her apartment at the Symphony and celebrate there.

Laura explained that the Symphony had an outdoor running track on the tenth floor that was open to all residents of the building. Which meant that on Thanksgiving, Laura and her guests could go out on the running track and look over the ledge to watch the big holiday floats coming down Broadway. They would get to see the floats *up close*! Just the thought made Maurice bubble with excitement and anticipation.

When Thanksgiving finally rolled around, Maurice put on his cleanest clothes and went over to Laura's apartment. Steve the doorman let Maurice right up. Laura's family was already in her apartment—Annette, Bruce, and their three children, plus Laura's other sister, Nancy, and her two brothers, Steven and Frank.

Maurice noticed an older man sitting on the sofa. He didn't know who he was, so he asked Laura.

"That's my father, Nunzie," she told him.

The same Nunzie from the stories Laura shared about her childhood!

124

Maurice asked Laura where her mother was.

"She passed away ten years ago," Laura said. "I really miss her."

Hearing this made Maurice think about someone in his family that he missed—his father, whom he hadn't seen since he walked out when Maurice was six years old.

Maurice noticed the smell of something wonderful cooking in the kitchen. That something, he understood, was the Thanksgiving turkey. From the incredible aroma wafting through the room, Maurice knew the turkey was going to be *delicious*.

"Okay, everyone," Laura announced, "the turkey will be ready a bit later. Let's go see the floats!"

Everyone jumped on elevators and rode them to the tenth floor. Maurice walked out on the running track and saw the tall buildings on Broadway spread out all around him. He was used to seeing them from ground level, but now he was up *among* them, staring down at the tiny people below. It was a crisp fall day and a cold wind blew across the track, but Maurice didn't care. Being so high up, with this view of the city, was simply spectacular.

"Look!" Maurice heard someone yell out. "There they are!"

Maurice joined everyone as they pressed against the ledge and looked up Broadway. In the distance, Maurice could see them—the Macy's floats! They were heading his way! The closer they got, the bigger and bigger they seemed. By the time they reached Fifty-Sixth Street, the floats were enormous! Maurice had expected them to be big, because even from street level they looked huge. But seeing them like this, passing right in front of his eyes, almost close enough to touch, was completely *magical*. Maurice just watched and took it all in—Snoopy, Raggedy Ann, Rocky and Bullwinkle, Superman. He found himself yelling and cheering along with Colette and Derek and Brooke and everyone else on the running track.

It was one of the most special moments of his life.

Laura's dinner table was smaller than the table in Annette's house, but everyone happily sat huddled together, laughing and talking about the floats. Laura and her sister Nancy brought out the food—a huge turkey, mounds of sweet potatoes and mashed potatoes, cranberry sauce, tons of gravy, and so much more. Somehow, they managed to squeeze all the plates on the table.

Everything looked so delicious, Maurice didn't know what to eat first. Once again he ate slowly, hoping to make the meal last longer. If he could have figured out a way to make it last forever, he would have.

After the meal Maurice went off to play with Derek and his sisters, while the adults sat around talking. At one point Maurice saw Nunzie heading toward him. He knew about Nunzie's angry side from what Laura had told him, so as Nunzie approached, Maurice didn't quite know what to expect.

But Maurice also knew that while his mother, Darcella, could be distant and neglectful when she was in the grips of her sickness, there were also times when she was sweet and loving. Her sickness didn't define her, and Maurice guessed the same was true of Nunzie.

That guess proved to be true. Nunzie came over to Maurice and gently put his hand on his shoulder.

"Are you having fun, Maurice?"

"Yes, sir," Maurice answered.

"Me too," Nunzie said. "Those floats were something, huh?"

"They were awesome," Maurice replied.

They spoke to each other about nothing special or important. They just shared the excitement of the day. But in that moment Nunzie seemed like a very kind and gentle man, and Maurice understood that Laura loved her father just as much as he loved his mother, because, in spite of their sicknesses, they were kind and gentle and loving people underneath.

When it was time for everyone to go, Laura gave Maurice a paper bag stuffed with Thanksgiving leftovers. There was enough turkey for Maurice to give plenty to his sisters and Grandma Rose, and even have more himself, if he got hungry again. Overall, Thanksgiving had turned into one of the most memorable days Maurice had ever had. For the first time he felt like he had actually "celebrated" something. Secretly, he wished his mother would be home at the Bryant when he got there, so he could share some of his special Thanksgiving Day with her.

He now understood that Thanksgiving was a day for people to sit down and think of all the things they were thankful for.

Laura told Maurice she had *so much* to be grateful for—her family, her friendships, her health, her job, her apartment, and on and on.

"I've been very, very blessed," she told him.

Laura didn't tell Maurice that he, too, should sit down and think of all the things he was thankful for. But just speaking with her about it made Maurice think about the ways he might have been blessed too. Sure enough, he thought of several things he could be thankful for.

He was thankful for his mother, and for all she had done, despite her sickness, to try to protect and care for him after Maurice's father left.

He was thankful for his sisters, LaToya and Celeste, who were silly and funny and could always make him laugh.

He was thankful for his uncles—Uncle Limp and Uncle Old and Uncle Juice. They weren't always there, and they didn't always pay that much attention to him, but sometimes they liked joking around with Maurice, and they could usually crack him up too.

He was thankful for Grandma Rose, who, despite her tough talk, clearly and dearly loved Maurice and told him how special he was.

Maurice was also thankful for all the people who had ever stopped and given him a quarter or nickel or dime on the street. To them, Maurice hadn't been invisible. For a brief, fleeting moment at least, they had stopped and seen Maurice for who he was—a human being, just like them.

And, of course, Maurice was thankful for Laura.

He was thankful she had turned around and come back to him on Broadway, and thankful she had taken him to McDonald's, and thankful she had agreed to meet him every Monday, and thankful for the brown paper bag lunches she made for him every day. He was thankful for all the amazing things she'd bought for him.

Most of all, Maurice was thankful for Laura's friendship.

Because even though Maurice was only eleven years old, he understood that her friendship was the most valuable gift Laura could ever give him.

Two weeks after Thanksgiving, during one of their Monday dinners, Laura asked Maurice what he and his family usually did for Christmas.

"Nothing," Maurice answered.

"Nothing? You mean you don't celebrate Christmas?"

"Nah," Maurice said.

That was true. It was possible Darcella had cooked fancy Christmas meals when Maurice was younger, but he couldn't remember them. For the past few years there had been no celebrations of any kind. The previous Christmas, when Maurice was ten, he went by himself to a Salvation Army in Brooklyn. He ate the free meal the Salvation Army offered on Christmas, and afterward someone led him and other kids over to a big cardboard bin that was half filled with toys for poor children.

"Go ahead, take one," the staffer told him.

Maurice reached in and pulled out a small white teddy bear with a little red heart on it. That was the closest he ever got to receiving a Christmas gift from anyone.

"Well, Maurice," Laura asked, "would you want to spend at least part of Christmas with me and my family?"

A big smile spread across Maurice's face. That was the only answer Laura needed.

15

THE SATURDAY BEFORE CHRISTMAS, Maurice met Laura to run a special errand. It was something he'd never had the chance to do before.

"We're going to pick out a Christmas tree!" Laura announced.

Every December tree farmers from upstate New York and neighboring states bundled up their blue spruces and Fraser firs and Scotch pines and other fine Christmas trees and trucked them into Manhattan, where they selected a street corner and strung some tarp and sold their trees to all the city people who couldn't cut down their own trees. There were different vendors every five or six blocks, and they all sold different sizes of trees starting at around twenty dollars. Maurice had noticed the vendors every Christmas season, but he'd never had any reason to stop and look at the trees. Until now.

Maurice and Laura found a vendor just three blocks from Laura's apartment, and together they picked a fresh and bushy Douglas fir. The vendor sawed two inches off the trunk and wrapped the tree tightly in green mesh. Then Laura and Maurice lugged it to her apartment, with Laura holding one end and Maurice the other. In the living room of Laura's apartment, Maurice helped her stand the tree up in a red plastic base and helped her tighten four screws to hold it in place.

"There," Laura said when they were done. "Now we're ready for the decorations."

Laura pulled a big cardboard box down from a closet shelf and set it on the floor in front of the tree. When she opened the box, Maurice looked at its contents with wonder. There were little red apple ornaments, and snowflakes, and strings of colored lights, and rows of silver tinsel. It was a dazzling display of everything that made Christmas so festive and fun—or at least how Maurice imagined Christmas.

Before they began decorating the tree, Laura made two cups of hot chocolate and warned Maurice to sip it slowly because it was hot. Then she went to her record player and put on an album of Christmas songs—"Silent Night," "Jingle Bells," "Rudolph the Red-Nosed Reindeer," and many more. Maurice knew most of the songs because he'd heard them playing over speakers outside of big stores like Macy's and Bloomingdale's. He sang along as they played in the living room. Laura wrapped the lights around the tree, and then, one by one, they took the ornaments out of the box and hung them from the branches.

Laura told Maurice that there was one special ornament she always saved for last—a beautiful silver heart that was engraved on one side with the word "Mom," and on the other side with the dates "April 6, 1929–October 13, 1976," the dates of Laura's mother's life. Maurice understood why the ornament was so special to Laura, and he watched as she hung it on a branch in a special place on the tree.

When they were done, they sat down on the sofa and admired the beautiful Christmas tree. There was more hot chocolate, and some chocolate chip cookies, and the Christmas songs were still playing. For Maurice, it was the first time in his life that he understood, even a tiny little bit, why Christmas was so special to everyone. It brought people together.

While they were sitting on the sofa, eating their cookies and watching the lights blink on and off, Laura handed Maurice a blank piece of paper.

"I want you to write down what you want Santa Claus to bring you this year," she said.

Maurice laughed. "There ain't no Santa Claus," he said.

"Of course there is a Santa Claus," Laura said, "so you need to make a list for him."

Maurice took a pencil and wrote down the only thing he could think of, the only present he really, truly wanted.

A remote-control race car.

Maurice had once seen someone playing with such a car on the sidewalk outside the Bryant, holding the remote control and steering the little car back and forth. He remembered how the race car made tight little turns and let out a noisy roar as it zipped around. It seemed like the coolest toy he could imagine.

But even as he wrote the words down, he never imagined having one of his own. After all, how would Santa Claus ever know where he lived? How else was he supposed to end up with such an expensive gift?

Maurice handed the paper back to Laura and asked her if they could sit on the sofa and look at the tree for a while longer. Maurice didn't want to let go of the happy feeling he had from the cookies and the hot chocolate and the Christmas carols and the warm glow of the Christmas tree lights. For a long time he and Laura sat without talking. Finally, Maurice spoke.

"Miss Laura, thank you for making my Christmas so nice," he said. "Kids like me—we know what's going on in the world. We see it in front of us, or on TV. But we're always on the outside looking in. We know about stuff like Christmas, but we also know that we can never have it for ourselves. It doesn't belong to us. We just choose not to think about it too much."

Across from Maurice, Laura looked a little sad.

"That's very wise of you, Maurice," she said. "But this Christmas *does* belong to you."

A few days later it was Christmas Eve. Laura invited Maurice to her apartment, and invited her sister Nancy, too. She seemed to like spending time with him. Maurice rode up the elevator to Laura's apartment, and Nancy was there to greet him at the door. When he went inside, the first thing he noticed was the Christmas tree. Well, not the tree, exactly, but what was underneath it.

There were eight or nine or ten presents wrapped in color-ful Christmas paper. Maurice had never seen so many Christ-mas presents all bunched together, except in the windows of department stores.

Laura caught Maurice eyeballing the Christmas tree and all the wrapped boxes and said, "Go ahead, Maurice, you can open one of your presents."

His presents?

First, it wasn't even Christmas Day. *Do people open presents on Christmas Eve?* Second, hearing someone say something was "his" was still a shock to Maurice—unless it was someone tell-ing him that something was "his" fault. The idea that some of the bright, beautiful boxes under the tree were *his* presents was almost more than he could comprehend.

Maurice sat down on the floor beside the tree and Laura handed him a box wrapped in bright red paper. He hesitated for a moment, not sure how to take the wrapping paper off without ruining it.

"Just rip it," Laura said.

But Maurice didn't want to rip it. It was too perfect. This would be the very *first* wrapped present of any kind he had ever received. The white teddy bear from the last Christmas hadn't been wrapped; he'd just plucked it out of a bin. But with this present, Laura had taken the time to carefully wrap it in colorful Christmas paper. She even attached a little tag that said, "To Maurice, From Santa Claus."

No, Maurice didn't want to rip the paper. Instead, he slowly and carefully pulled it apart, until he could see what was inside.

It was a brand-new remote-control race car.

Up until then, Laura had given Maurice many "presents," but they had always been practical things—socks, T-shirts, shirts and pants, things he needed. But this present, this race car—this was different. This was something Maurice *wanted*. And, suddenly, as if by magic, it was right there in his hands. It was *his*.

As he held his new race car and marveled at its sleekness, Maurice didn't know what to say. He couldn't think of the right words to express how grateful he was for the present. After a while of trying to find the right words, Maurice gave up. "Thank you, Miss Laura."

"You're welcome, Maurice," she replied. "Now let's make it race!"

While Laura got dinner ready, Nancy helped Maurice assemble the race car and put in the batteries. When they were done, Nancy handed the remote control to Maurice. There wasn't much room in Laura's apartment, but that didn't stop Maurice from starting the race car and steering it down the hallway, under the dinner table, into the bathroom, back out to the living room, and finally straight into the kitchen, where Laura was cooking. Then Maurice picked up the race car and put it down by the Christmas tree and raced it on the same loop all over again. Every few minutes Laura would come out of the kitchen just to see the look of sheer joy on Maurice's face, but he didn't notice. He was too busy playing with his new race car.

"Miss Laura, can I bring my present to Annette's house tomorrow for Christmas?" Maurice asked. "I want to show it to Derek."

"Of course," Laura said.

Maurice wondered, if Christmas Eve had been this much fun, how great would Christmas Day be?

It turned out even greater than Maurice had hoped.

When he walked into Annette's house on Christmas morning, Maurice couldn't help but notice the Christmas tree in her living room. It was *huge*. It had to be twice the size of Laura's tree! And beneath this magnificent Christmas tree lay Christmas presents—not just two or three, or even eight or nine, but probably a *hundred*! Could all these presents possibly be just for one family? It almost didn't seem real.

The rest of Annette's house was covered with Christmas decorations—wreaths, tinsel, a wooden manger with little figurines, fake snow sprayed on the glass doors, colorful lights. It was nearly as expansive and dazzling as the Christmas displays Maurice had seen in the famous windows of the Saks Fifth Avenue department store. Maurice walked around Annette's house in something like a daze. It felt like he'd stumbled into a Christmas wonderland, and he never wanted to leave.

Before long, Annette announced it was time for everyone to gather by the Christmas tree and open their presents. Maurice had already received his present the night before, so he wasn't expecting to get anything else on Christmas Day. But as soon as everyone had found a space around the tree, Annette asked Colette to pick out a present and hand it to the person whose name was on the tag. Colette picked a box wrapped in bright green paper and walked over and handed it to Maurice.

"Merry Christmas, Maurice," Colette said.

Maurice was stunned. Another present? Once again he carefully took off the wrapping paper until he could see what was inside. He knew what it was right away, but even so, it took him a few moments to actually process what he was seeing, as if it was too good to be true.

It was a beautiful, brand-new, bright orange basketball.

And now it was "his" basketball.

"Can I see?" Derek asked him.

Maurice handed the ball to Derek, who seemed just as excited as he was to hold it.

"This is so cool," Derek said.

The basketball was just the first of many presents Maurice received that day. He also got a nice new Tommy Hilfiger shirt, a new pair of gloves, new white sneakers, a warm winter jacket, a scarf, and other wonderful little gifts. By the time everyone had opened their presents, Maurice was completely overwhelmed. He felt incredibly happy, but a part of him also felt a little confused. He'd never been showered with gifts like this, and he wasn't sure how to react. He didn't even know which of his presents to pick up and play with first.

And, of course, he couldn't help but remember what his mother and Grandma Rose had always warned—*No one does nothing for nothing. Everyone wants something from you, so don't trust no one. There is us, and there is them.*

What did all these presents mean? Why were these people so nice to him when they didn't really even know him? Were they being nice just because they wanted to? Was that how the world really worked? People loving and trusting one another and giving one another gifts?

Maurice didn't know what to think. But instead of worrying about it too much, he asked Derek if he wanted to play with his new race car, and the two of them ran off and raced it up and down a long hallway. For a moment, at least, Maurice felt all his worries and warnings and fears melt away, and in their place all he felt was happy.

And in that beautiful moment when all he had to worry about was steering his race car as fast as he could, Maurice had one simple thought.

This must be what a normal kid feels like.

After a while Annette summoned everyone to the dining room, and once again everyone sat around the big table. Annette and Bruce were each at the end of the table and on one side was Nunzio, Steven, Colette, and Brooke and on the other side was Frank, Nancy, Laura, Maurice, and Derek. The only person missing was their mom, Marie. They held hands and said grace, and shared a meal that was delicious and plentiful, and stayed in their chairs long afterward to talk and laugh. And after dinner Annette handed out sheet music that had the words to a few Christmas songs printed on them, and everyone sat around singing Christmas carols together while Steven played the organ. When it got late, Nancy helped Laura load all Maurice's presents into the car for the ride back into New York City. Maurice agreed to keep them all at Laura's place, where he knew they would be safe, and where he could play with them whenever he came over.

Maurice thanked Laura for his remarkable day and ran back to the Bryant hotel. When he entered his apartment, nothing was different. Grandma Rose was in her chair, and his sisters, LaToya and Celeste, were in the bed. His mother and uncles were nowhere to be seen. Maurice handed his sisters a large bag with some of the clothes Laura no longer needed and the plates of leftovers Annette had packed for him. Even Grandma Rose got some Christmas turkey that night.

When Maurice finally went into his closet, exhausted from the day but too excited to sleep, he had one overriding thought.

It wasn't about all the presents he received.

Or the giant turkey Bruce had carved at the big dinner table.

It didn't include the Christmas songs they'd all happily sung together.

No. Maurice thought about something he had left behind in Laura's apartment.

It was something he had sneaked into her apartment on Christmas morning, before they took the drive to Annette's house on Long Island. Maurice had hidden it underneath his sweatshirt so no one would see him carrying it. And then, when no one was looking, Maurice had put it underneath the Christmas tree in Laura's living room.

Since everyone was so busy getting ready to go to Annette's house, neither Laura nor Nancy had noticed it sitting under the tree. But Maurice knew that once Laura was by herself in her apartment, she would sit on the sofa with her hot chocolate and notice it.

She would see that Maurice had given her the only present he had in the world to give her.

His stuffed white teddy bear with the little red heart.

And along with the gift, she would find a note that Maurice had written himself.

"Merry Christmas, Miss Laura," she would read. "Thank you for being my friend."

16

MAURICE AND LAURA KEPT meeting every Monday for a long time. After a while Maurice lost track of how long they'd been having dinner together, but one day Laura told him it was almost four years. That was more than two hundred Mondays! And in that time Laura had kept her promise to Maurice—that all she wanted from him was to be friends. She had also kept her promise to his teacher, Miss House—that she would always be there for Maurice, and that she would never abandon him.

Laura and Maurice did many different things. One Monday Laura announced they were going to bake a cake, and in her kitchen Laura showed Maurice the recipe they would be using. Maurice didn't know what a recipe was.

"How come you can't just throw all that stuff in there together?" he asked.

"Because then you won't know what you'll end up with," Laura explained. "If you want something to be good, you have to put the right ingredients in at the right time."

Laura showed Maurice how the recipe worked. She let him pour a tiny bit of vanilla extract onto a teaspoon, then drop the liquid into the cake batter. She taught Maurice how to properly stir the batter. At each step, Laura explained what she was doing and why it was important.

"It's about discipline and being accurate," Laura said, using two words Maurice didn't understand. "That means being focused and careful, and working hard on getting everything just right."

It was another one of those moments when Maurice got the idea that Laura was trying to teach him a lesson—and that the lesson wasn't just about baking.

But that was okay with Maurice, because once the cake was baked, he and Laura let it cool and covered it in chocolate frosting, and Laura even let Maurice eat some of the frosting right off the big wooden spoon. Maurice ate it and thought, *This is a pretty delicious way to learn a lesson.*

Another time, Maurice asked Laura how she was going to spend all the change in the big plastic jug she kept in her apartment. Maurice had been curious about all the change in the jug from the minute he'd first seen it. He guessed there were a thousand quarters in the jug, not to mention hundreds of dimes, nickels, and pennies. Why was Laura collecting all that change if she wasn't going to spend it on something?

"I'm saving that money for when I might need it," Laura explained.

Maurice wasn't sure what she meant by "saving." Having

money and not spending it was not a familiar concept for Maurice. In his world, when people got money, they spent it. Right away. But here was Laura, sitting on a fortune! Why, he asked, was she "saving" it?

"I don't know. Maybe I'll decide to buy a nice new car someday," Laura said. "Or maybe I'll use it to help buy a little house. Or maybe I'll put it in the bank and hold on to it in case I need it for an emergency. That's what savings are for, Maurice. You save your money for when you really need it."

Maurice still didn't quite understand. In his world, people really needed money *all the time*.

Even so, Maurice understood that Laura had used the big jug of loose change to teach him not one but *two* life lessons.

The first was about savings. If you were smart, you could plan for the future and even control it, and not just let it happen to you.

The second lesson was about trust.

There were times when Maurice had thought about taking a few coins out of the jug, so he could use them at the arcade to play Asteroids or buy food. There were so many quarters, Maurice told himself, Laura would never miss them. But even though he was tempted, he never came close to taking any of her coins. He remembered what Laura had told him—that they were friends, and that friendships were based on trust. Maurice had agreed to their friendship pact, and even shaken hands on it.

And because of that, he realized that the fun he might have playing Asteroids or eating a Big Mac was not nearly as important or meaningful to him as Laura's friendship. So he made the right choice and stayed away from the jug.

Sometimes Laura would say something to Maurice that sounded like an actual lesson, instead of a lesson hidden inside a cake-baking night. One time Laura told Maurice that he needed to always be "a straight arrow." Maurice wasn't sure what that meant, so he asked Laura to explain.

"Being a straight arrow means always asking yourself, 'What is the right thing to do in this situation?' and then doing that thing," she said. "It means always picking the smart and honest course of action, and then sticking to it, no matter what temptations might arise to try to lead you off it. It means sticking to your plan, even if bad things might happen. And the way you manage to stay on the right course—the way you become a straight arrow—is through focus, courage, and perseverance."

Maurice didn't understand everything Laura told him. But he understood a lot of it, and he kept it stored away for the future.

One Saturday morning Maurice looked around his apartment and saw that everyone was gone except Grandma Rose. He figured his mother and his uncles and sisters were out somewhere, doing whatever they were doing. Then he saw Grandma Rose's face, and instantly he knew something was wrong.

"What is it, Grandma?" he asked her.

"Your mother got arrested," Rose said. "She's on Rikers Island."

Maurice felt a terrible sense of dread and fear. He had heard the grown-ups talk about a prison called Rikers Island, and about how it was a really horrible place to be. It wasn't safe, they'd say, and you could get really hurt. And now his mother was there! Maurice was beginning to panic. He wanted to save his mother, but he didn't know what to do.

"Grandma, we got to do something," Maurice said.

"Ain't nothing we can do," Rose said. "She'll get out soon enough."

But that answer wasn't good enough for Maurice. He didn't want to wait around until his mother got out of Rikers. He wanted to do something to help her *right away*. The reality was, Grandma Rose was right—there wasn't anything they could do. Still, he had to try. He ran out of the apartment and ran out onto the street, and even though it wasn't a Monday, he ran to Laura's apartment.

The doorman let Maurice up, and Laura was waiting for him at the door of her apartment. When she saw him, she knew something was wrong.

"Maurice, what is it?" she asked.

"My mom got arrested," he said. "She's in jail. She's on Rikers Island. Miss Laura, I know Rikers is a really bad place where really bad things happen. What am I gonna do?"

Laura sat Maurice down at the dinner table and brought him a glass of orange juice. Then she sat with him at the table and let him talk about all the thoughts and feelings running through his mind. For the first time Maurice shared everything about his mother with Laura. He told her about his mother's sickness, and how it made her act, and how much he wished she could get better, but that he also understood that she still loved him.

And as he shared everything with Laura, he noticed Laura didn't say much in return. She just listened and let Maurice talk. She didn't offer any easy solutions, and Maurice realized it was because there *were* no easy solutions. There was nothing he could do but wait for his mother to be released and hope that nothing bad happened to her.

Even so, it felt good to be able to share his feelings with someone. Being able to talk about his mother made Maurice feel less afraid. Laura had somehow brought him comfort just by listening. It occurred to Maurice that this was the first time in his life when he had someone to turn to with a problem. And he understood a little better what "friendship" truly meant.

Maurice's mother stayed in prison for the next several months. Maurice would get word from his uncles and from Grandma Rose that Darcella was doing fine and nothing bad had happened, and that made him feel a little better. He still didn't know what she had done wrong to deserve being sent to prison, but it didn't matter anyway. All Maurice wanted was for his mother to come home.

Darcella was still in prison when Maurice's birthday rolled around in April. Laura asked if she could throw him a birthday party since his mother couldn't. Then she surprised him one Monday evening by handing him a white envelope.

"Go ahead, see what's inside," Laura told him.

Maurice opened the envelope and saw two tickets. They were tickets to WrestleMania at Madison Square Garden.

WrestleMania! Maurice couldn't believe it! Next to baseball, his favorite thing in the world was professional wrestling, which he sometimes got to watch on the storefront TVs. He had told Laura all about his heroes in the World Wrestling Federation—Hulk Hogan, Rowdy Roddy Piper, Randy Savage, Ricky Steamboat. Maurice loved to copy their moves and pretend he was in the ring wrestling an opponent, even if he was by himself. But to actually get to see his favorite wrestlers in Madison Square Garden? Up close? That was something he never dreamed could actually happen.

It turned out to be a really special night. Laura bought them amazing seats, and Maurice got to see all his heroes from just a few dozen feet away. It was electrifying! There were several different wrestling matches that went on for more than two hours, and in that time Maurice hardly stopped yelling and screaming. Like everyone else in the arena, he was caught up in the excitement and couldn't help himself. It was the most fun he could ever remember having, outside of watching the Mets, and by the end of it he could barely talk.

But WrestleMania was only half his birthday surprise. The following Sunday, Laura drove Maurice out to Annette's house and threw a party for him. In the middle of the party, Laura told Maurice that they had to go to a nearby store to pick up a new bicycle that Bruce had bought for Derek. Maurice went along and marveled at all the new bicycles standing in a long row at the store. They were so beautiful. They had shiny black tires, and they were painted bright colors, and their handlebars were curved and sleek. How lucky Derek was, Maurice thought, to be able to have this kind of bicycle for himself.

Suddenly, the manager of the store came out from a back room. He was pushing a new bicycle with a big red bow tied around it. It was a Ross chrome ten-speeder, and it was the coolest bike Maurice had ever seen. The manager wheeled the bicycle over to where Maurice was standing with Derek and Bruce and Laura and the whole family. Then he kicked the brake stand and left the bicycle right in front of Maurice.

"Congratulations on your new bike, kid," the manager said.

Maurice was confused, and he pointed at Derek.

"No, that's for him," he said.

And then all at once, Bruce and Annette and Derek and Colette and Brooke and Laura and Nancy and Steven yelled, "*SURPRISE!*"

Why were they yelling at him?

"It's yours," Laura finally told him. "Happy birthday, Maurice."

Maurice didn't know what to say.

Maurice and Derek spent the next hours riding their bikes around the neighborhood. Even when Annette called them in for dinner, Maurice didn't want to stop riding. He wanted to keep riding his new bike forever, and maybe even longer.

Maurice agreed to keep his new bicycle in the bike room at Laura's building. He knew that if he brought it with him to the Bryant, it wouldn't be around for long. If he wanted to ride it, all he had to do was run up to Laura's building and ask Steve to let him into the bike room to fetch it. The only condition, Laura had told Maurice, was that he needed to be careful about where he rode, and he always had to have it back in the bike room before nighttime. Maurice understood. There were a lot of places in New York City where it wouldn't be safe to ride—where someone might steal your bike right from underneath you.

Maurice was very careful. He mostly bicycled around the block on Fifty-Fourth Street, though sometimes he would stray a little farther west, toward Eighth Avenue. Maurice *never* got tired of riding his bike. Riding his bike made him feel *free*. Whipping down busy streets or through Central Park, with the wind blowing in his face, was exciting—it was one of the best feelings he could imagine. Maurice soon decided that of all the amazing things Laura and her family had bought for him, the Ross ten-speeder was his very favorite gift. He loved his new bicycle in a way he had never loved anything before.

One summer afternoon Maurice raced his bicycle around the block ten or twelve times without stopping, until he felt totally exhausted. He finally hit the brakes on the corner of Fifty-Fourth Street and Seventh Avenue just to rest and catch his breath. While he was sitting on his bicycle, he noticed a man walking toward him. The man was in his twenties, and Maurice knew his face from around the neighborhood. They had never spoken, but it was clear that the man recognized Maurice from the Bryant.

"Nice bike," the man said. "Can I take it for a spin?"

"No," Maurice said quickly.

"Come on, little man, just a quick spin," the man said. "I'll take it around the corner and back. I just want to try it out."

Once again Maurice said, "No."

"Little man, I'm not gonna steal your bike," he said. "If you don't trust me, how about this. I'll let you hold my driver's license while I ride your bike. That way you know I have to come back for it."

The man reached into his wallet, took out his driver's license, and held it out toward Maurice.

Maurice did not want to let the man ride his new bike. His instinct was to pedal away as fast as he could. But then a different instinct took hold. It was an instinct Maurice had never felt before, at least not until he met Laura.

Maurice felt the instinct to *trust*.

And so Maurice stepped off his bike and took the driver's license. He watched the man get on the bicycle and start pedaling.

"I'll be back in five minutes!" the man yelled as he sped away.

Maurice sat down on a building stoop and waited.

Five minutes passed, and the man hadn't returned. Maurice waited some more. Ten minutes. Fifteen minutes. Half an hour.

It was getting dark outside, and still the man hadn't come back.

Maurice looked at the driver's license. He noticed the photo didn't even look like the man who took his bicycle. And it didn't look real, either. The license was probably a fake.

Which meant the man was never coming back.

Even so, Maurice stayed on the stoop and waited, hoping to see his Ross ten-speeder again.

Maurice waited for seven hours. He knew his bike was gone forever.

17

MAURICE DIDN'T TELL LAURA the truth about his bicycle. He told her that two boys had knocked him off the bike and had stolen it from him. Maurice didn't want to tell her that he had trusted a stranger to come back with his bike; it was embarrassing. He was mad at himself for being so trusting. Looking back on it, he realized it was a stupid thing to do. Yes, Laura was teaching him lessons about relationships and trust and being a straight arrow, but those lessons didn't always apply on the streets. The streets had their own set of rules and lessons, and ignoring them could lead to very bad things.

"I'm so sorry, Maurice," Laura told him. "The main thing is you weren't hurt. The bicycle is just an object; it can be replaced, but you cannot."

But both Laura and Maurice understood—even if they didn't say it—that to Maurice, the bicycle was more than just a "thing." It represented something important; it was *his* and it had been a gift from Laura, someone who seemed to really care about him. While it was literally just a *thing*, it represented something much more meaningful. Maurice never told Laura how truly devastating it was for him to lose his bicycle. Around her, he just shrugged it off and pretended like it didn't really matter.

Then, a few days after his bicycle was stolen, on one of his regular Mondays with Laura, Maurice received another shock.

Maurice didn't know that much about Laura's personal life. He knew she had a job, and she worked at *USA Today*, and he knew most of her family. He was aware she wasn't married, and that she sometimes went out on dates. But that was about it—until that night.

Laura had met a really nice man named Michael. She said Michael was warm and funny, kind, gracious, and sophisticated, and she told Maurice that she really liked him.

"That's great, Miss Laura," Maurice said.

Over the following Mondays, Laura kept Maurice up-to-date on her relationship with Michael, and on how they were growing closer. A few months after Laura and Michael met, Laura met Maurice for dinner and said she had something to tell him.

From her tone of voice, Maurice could tell it was serious and he braced himself for the worst.

"Maurice," Laura said, "I'm going to be moving away."

Maurice tried hard not to act too surprised, but inside he was shocked. Having Laura move away wasn't anything he'd ever thought would happen. He just assumed their Mondays would go on forever.

Laura explained that she and Michael were in love, and

they were planning to get married. In the meantime, Laura said, Michael had asked her to move into his home in Westchester and she said yes. Westchester, she explained, was a county about thirty miles north of New York City. It's where people who had finally had enough of city living bought houses. The neighborhoods there were quiet and full of trees and parks and churches and nice little stores.

As she was explaining all this to Maurice, he could tell that she was sad about leaving. She looked like she might even start to cry.

"Miss Laura," Maurice said, "I am so happy for you. I really am."

"Westchester is only about a forty-minute drive away, so we'll still be able to see each other every Monday, same as always," Laura said. "It's just that on the other days, well, I won't be around."

And then Laura did start to cry.

Maurice knew Laura was sad about leaving the city. And maybe she was even sad that, most likely, she would be seeing Maurice less often than when they lived so near to each other. Maybe, Maurice thought, Miss House's words were playing in Laura's head—*You can't just wake up one day and abandon this boy.* Maybe that's what made Laura cry. He didn't know how to make it better; deep down, he was really sad too.

"Miss Laura, we'll still see each other on Mondays," Maurice said. "We can still go to the Hard Rock Cafe. Everything will be just the same."

"I know," Laura said, wiping away her tears. "It's just that . . ." Laura trailed off before finishing her sentence.

"Miss Laura, it's okay," Maurice said. "Don't worry about me. I'm gonna be just fine. And, anyway, this is your time now, Miss Laura. This is the time for you to be happy and get everything you want."

A month later Laura packed up all her belongings, and moved out of New York City. Up until then, she and Maurice had lived only two short blocks apart. Now they were separated by many miles.

To Maurice, the streets suddenly felt different. The corner of Fifty-Sixth Street felt different. The arcade on Broadway felt different.

He had told Laura that everything would stay the same.

But that was another lie.

At the same time that Laura was planning to move out of the city, something else was happening in Maurice's life that made the sadness of Laura moving away feel a little less sad.

One evening his mother, Darcella, called Maurice over.

"Your momma's been given her own apartment in Brooklyn," she proudly said.

Maurice could hardly believe his ears. He knew that over the years his mother had applied for what was known as Section 8 housing, a federal program that set aside and rented apartments to low-income families. Darcella had never been awarded an apartment, but now, all of a sudden, she had one.

"Do you know what that means, Maurice?" Darcella said. "It means we're going to have our own home. Our very own apartment."

It almost seemed too good to be true, but it *was* true. And as it turned out, Maurice's family was moving to Brooklyn the very same weekend that Laura was moving to Westchester. For the first time in his young life, Maurice was going to live in a place that wasn't a shelter or a welfare hotel or someone else's room. He would live in an apartment that was just for him and his family.

"And, baby," Darcella told him, "you and the girls will even have your very own room."

Maurice reached out and gave his mother a hug. He hugged her tight, and he hugged her for a long time. She seemed different too. Her sickness wasn't affecting her in the same bad way. She was alert and happy. She was like the person Maurice always knew was under there somewhere, beneath all the layers of sickness.

Maurice slept in his closet that night, excited by the idea that he wouldn't need to sleep in a closet in his family's new apartment. He would have a room that he shared with his sisters, and he would even have his own bed. It *still* felt too good to be true, and Maurice had to keep reminding himself that it was, indeed, true.

Before he knew it, it was Friday. Moving day.

"If you ever need to speak with me about anything," Laura said, "you have my phone number, and you can call me collect."

Maurice gave her a big hug, happy in the knowledge that he would see Laura again that very Monday, same as always.

Darcella had told Maurice and his sisters they should pack up their things and be ready to leave for their new apartment that evening. She was going out for the day, to take care of some business, but when she came back, the whole family would leave their room in the Bryant for good, and head out to Brooklyn.

The hours couldn't pass quickly enough. Maurice had packed his few items of clothing, including some of the nice new things Laura had given him, into a plastic bag. Every few minutes Maurice would check the watch around his neck to see what time it was. His mother said she'd be back home around five p.m. But five p.m. came and went with no sign of Darcella. *That's okay. She must be running a little late.*

Maurice kept checking his watch: Five fifteen, five thirty, five forty. By six, his mother still hadn't returned.

"Where do you think she is?" he asked Grandma Rose.

"She's on the way," Rose said. "Just hush and be patient."

Maurice kept waiting. Now it was seven. Then eight. Nighttime had fallen, and still no sign of Darcella. Maurice sat on the floor near the front door and kept waiting, and he waited so long that he even fell asleep for a while. When he woke up, he checked his watch again, and now it said eleven thirty p.m. Maurice waited a few more minutes, then went to sleep in his closet.

By the next morning his mother still hadn't come home.

Grandma Rose had no idea where she was either. Maurice kept expecting his mother to come through the door at any moment and say, "Okay, everyone, let's get this show on the road!" But hour after hour, it seemed less likely. Maurice's mother didn't come home all day Saturday, or Saturday night, either. She was missing on Sunday as well.

Finally, on Monday, one of Maurice's uncles, Uncle Big, came into the apartment with news. He whispered it to Grandma Rose, then left.

"What is it?" Maurice asked his grandmother. "Where's Momma?"

"She been arrested," Rose said. "We got to go see her in court."

As usual, Maurice didn't know why his mother had been arrested again. Later that day he overheard two of his uncles talking about some kind of fight. Maurice didn't know if his mother started the fight, or if someone else did, or if she was hurt, or anything at all. All he knew was that his mother was scheduled to appear in a Brooklyn courtroom, in front of a judge, that Monday. But even though Maurice didn't know any of the details of what had happened to his mother, he knew enough to guess that it had something to do with her sickness.

Maurice also knew that he wouldn't be allowed to go to court with the adults. That afternoon another of Maurice's uncles, Uncle Juice, came by and picked up Grandma Rose and took her to the courtroom in Brooklyn.

A few hours later, when Grandma Rose came back home, she told Maurice what happened.

Grandma Rose said that she watched Maurice's mother, Darcella, walk into the courtroom wearing an orange jumpsuit. Maurice knew that was what prisoners wore. Darcella's hands were connected by handcuffs.

Darcella sat down at a table in front of the courtroom, and a well-dressed woman sitting next to her stood and addressed the judge, an old man in a black robe sitting behind a big bench. "Your Honor, this woman's family has been homeless for several years, and they have lived in subhuman shelters for most of their lives," the woman said. "They finally have a chance to have an apartment of their own. Could you please have mercy on this mother and on her family, and dismiss this case, and let them have this one chance at living a normal life?"

The old man behind the big desk frowned.

"What about the woman your client was in a fight with?" he asked.

"My client was simply defending herself," the woman said.

"I don't believe it," the old man said.

Then, just like that, Darcella was back on her feet and being led out of the courtroom by the armed guard. She didn't even have the chance to turn around and see Grandma Rose, and maybe smile at her or wave good-bye. She just vanished.

"The judge didn't dismiss the case," Grandma Rose explained to him. "Your momma has to go to trial. That means she has to stay in jail for now."

"But what about our new apartment?" Maurice asked.

"The new apartment?" Rose said. "That's gone now. Might as well put it out of your head."

Maurice felt like someone had just knocked him to the ground.

All along Maurice had been afraid that moving into a new apartment was too good to be true. And all along he'd been right. Some other lucky family would get to move into it now. Meanwhile, Maurice's mother had to stay in jail until her trial started, and that was weeks away. Grandma Rose explained to Maurice that his mother was in serious trouble and might be kept in jail for many years.

"With a good lawyer," Rose told him, "she might be able to get out in two years."

Two years! Darcella had never spent that long in prison. Could it possibly be true that Maurice would lose his mother for that long? The idea of Darcella being locked away was too terrible for Maurice to think about, so he pushed the thought out of his mind and tried to think about anything else.

It wasn't easy. He couldn't help but think about where she was, and how she was doing. If people were nice to her. If she was scared.

And there was another problem. Because Darcella had already signed on to take the new apartment in Brooklyn, her family's place in the Bryant Hotel had already been given to another family. Maurice, his sisters, and Grandma Rose would have to leave.

That night Maurice met Laura at their usual spot on Fifty-Sixth Street. It was their first time meeting since Laura had moved out three days earlier. Right after Maurice had learned his mother was arrested, he remembered what Laura had told him—*if you need to speak with me, call me collect*. So Maurice did. Laura did her very best to comfort him, and kept assuring him that everything would be okay.

But what Maurice didn't tell Laura during the phone call, or even on Monday night when they met, was that his family had lost the Brooklyn apartment Darcella had been promised. And he didn't tell her that he had to move out of the Bryant. He let Laura believe he was still going to be living in a nice apartment in Brooklyn. Maurice didn't want Laura to feel bad about the terrible turn his life had taken. She had her own life to worry about.

Finally, Maurice got a little bit of good news. Some New York City official had taken pity on Grandma Rose and awarded *her* an apartment in Brooklyn through the Section 8 program. It wouldn't be the same as moving into his own apartment, but at least Maurice had someplace to go. Just two weeks after his mother's arrest, Maurice finally moved out of the Bryant for good.

When he and his sisters and Grandma Rose arrived at her new apartment, Maurice was surprised by how small it was. There were two rooms instead of just one, but both rooms were pretty cramped. There was no furniture, and the floors and walls were dirty. There was also a funny smell coming from the radiator. But Maurice had seen worse, and lived in worse. He was thankful that he had a roof over his head at all.

The only problem was that the news of Grandma Rose's apartment spread. Three of his uncles came by, and so did several other people Maurice didn't even know. Just as he used to do at the Bryant, Maurice silently counted the people in the apartment. One, two, three, four, five . . . ten.

No wait, eleven.

Twelve.

There were twelve people staying with Grandma Rose. There was even less room for Maurice and his sisters than there had been in the Bryant.

But what could Maurice do? He had nowhere else to go. The constant stream of people coming and going, the loud noises and the lack of food and the dirty floors and walls, nothing was any better. And, of course, the absence of the person he loved most in the entire world—his mother.

For a few days it seemed to Maurice that he had no choice but to stay put and make the best of his bad situation.

But then, on one particularly bad and noisy day, when Grandma Rose's apartment was so crowded with people that Maurice could hardly find a place to sit or stand, he had another thought.

Maurice was fifteen years old now. He wasn't a kid anymore. He was practically all grown up. And now he faced a decision that was definitely a grown-up's decision: Was it time to strike out on his own?

Maurice had spent so much of his life on the streets. He understood the streets. They were where he really belonged.

Maurice decided he would run away from his grandmother's apartment and start living in the only real home he knew.

18

EVEN AFTER MAURICE LEFT his grandmother's apartment, he continued to meet Laura on Monday evenings at their old familiar spot.

During dinner Laura would tell Maurice about how things were going in Westchester, and she would ask him about his new apartment and his life in Brooklyn.

But Maurice wasn't exactly truthful.

"It's okay," is all he would say. If Laura asked how his mother was doing in prison, Maurice would say, "She's doing fine," even though he had no idea if she was. He never told her the truth about his life on the streets.

And the truth was—it was hard.

Right after Laura left the city, Maurice continued going to school. Not every day, but two or three times a week. But after a while, and especially when he was living on his own, he stopped going altogether. He just didn't see the point of being there anymore. He never told Laura that he dropped out, and when she asked him how school was going, he'd say it was going great okay. He didn't like lying to Laura, but he told himself it was better than dumping all his problems on her.

When he first decided to leave his grandmother's apartment, Maurice had a plan in place. He would spend his days on the street, asking strangers for loose change. He would use that money to eat, and hopefully have enough left over to buy a ticket to get into the Times Square Theater on Forty-Second Street. It was an old, run-down theater that stayed open twenty-four hours and showed kung fu movies around the clock. Most people called it the Kung Fu Theater. Maurice could take a seat in the back of the theater, curl up in the seat, and sleep there. It was noisy, with all the loud sounds coming from the movie, so it wasn't the perfect place to try to sleep. But Maurice was used to noise. Plus, it was always dark and no one ever bothered him in the back row. No one even knew he was there.

In the mornings he'd wake up and hit the streets again.

Every few days he would sneak into the YMCA on the west side to take a quick shower and clean himself up. And on good days, when he made more money asking for change than he needed, he would buy a ticket to get into the theater across the street from the Kung Fu Theater. It was showing his favorite movie—*Coming to America* with Eddie Murphy. Maurice watched the movie over and over, partly because he loved it, partly because he had nowhere to go and nothing to do.

Once in a while Maurice would travel back to Brooklyn to check up on Grandma Rose and his sisters. By then Maurice's sisters were old enough to take care of themselves and move out of Grandma Rose's apartment, but, still, Maurice wanted to make sure they were doing okay. He would also ask Grandma Rose if she had any news about his mother. Grandma Rose and Maurice's sisters went to see Darcella in prison once a month, but Maurice never went with them. He didn't want to. Seeing her there would only remind him that she couldn't be part of his life anymore, at least until she got out.

In reality, there were just things about his life and his world that Laura would never really understand.

For instance, Laura had always told Maurice that if he worked hard and stayed focused, he could overcome the difficulties of his childhood and make a better life for himself when he grew up. And Maurice believed her.

But then he would learn different lessons from the people in his world. Once, Maurice was talking to a man he knew from around the Bryant Hotel. Maurice told him that one day he hoped to have a family and a home of his own.

"You?" the man said. "You got to be joking. If you keep living this way, you'll be dead before you turn eighteen. Either dead or in jail."

The man knew what he was talking about. He had seen plenty of kids who grew up like Maurice end up dead or in jail. Who was Maurice supposed to believe? A man who understood what happened to people in his world, or Laura?

Maurice had only a few years to go before he turned eighteen. He began to wonder if he would ever get there.

Maurice quickly realized he had to find a better way to make money than by begging for it on the street. He didn't want to have to do that anymore. He was old enough to get a job now. He knew someone who had a job as a messenger—someone who delivers packages to offices all over New York City. Maurice figured he could do that kind of job. He knew the streets well, and he was young and fast, and he could deliver packages more quickly than other, older messengers. He might even become the fastest messenger in all of Manhattan.

Maurice went back to Grandma Rose's apartment and got the cleanest clothes he had. Then he went to a messenger agency and asked if there were any jobs, but the manager told him there were no openings. Maurice heard the very same thing from the manager at the next agency he visited. Then he heard the same response at the third. Maurice began to wonder if they could tell he was homeless and lived on the streets, and maybe they didn't want to hire someone like that. Maybe finding a job was going to be a lot harder than he thought.

Luckily, the manager of the fourth messenger service he visited—Bullet Messenger Manpower—took a liking to him.

"Tell you what, kid," the man said. "I'll take a chance on you."

Just like that, Maurice was hired to be a messenger. His job was to pick up letters and files and documents and packages from one office in Manhattan and deliver them to another office as quickly as possible. It was hard work, but Maurice didn't mind. Now instead of asking strangers for change every day, he spent the day outside and earned a paycheck.

No one in Maurice's immediate family had ever earned a paycheck before him.

Maurice's salary was eight dollars an hour. Most days he worked about ten hours, which meant he made around eighty dollars a day. To Maurice, that was a fortune! On his very best days asking for change, he might make eight dollars all day. For the first time in his life, Maurice had enough money to feed himself, and to even buy a new pair of pants or a shirt if he needed to. He didn't have enough to pay for a place to live and sleep, at least not yet. But working as a messenger and earning a paycheck gave Maurice a sense of freedom and accomplishment that he'd never had before. It was a wonderful feeling.

And all along, Maurice remembered the values Laura tried to instill in him: Be a straight arrow. Work hard. Stay focused. Persevere.

Earning eight dollars an hour had another effect on Maurice. It made him want to earn even more. He didn't want to just survive. He wanted to earn more freedom and more opportunities to create a better life. While he worked as a messenger, he kept his eye open for other chances to earn more money.

One day, when Maurice went back to visit Grandma Rose, she had a surprise for him.

"Your momma's getting out of prison," Rose said.

It had been two years since his mother got arrested and

sent away. Now she was getting out. But that wasn't the only good news. Grandma Rose explained that Darcella had also been awarded her own Section 8 apartment again in Brooklyn. And she wanted her children to live with her.

To Maurice, it was the best news he could ever hope to hear.

As soon as his mother was set up in her new apartment, Maurice moved back home. Seeing his mother again was incredible. She looked thinner, but she also looked healthier. She was alert and happy. It was like her sickness just went away. Best of all, Darcella didn't allow anyone else to stay there, so it was only the two of them—Maurice and his mother. To Maurice, it felt like the first time they could truly be a family. And it meant Maurice didn't have to sleep in the Kung Fu Theater anymore, or sneak into the YMCA to clean himself up.

He had a home now.

Everything worked out well for the first few weeks, until the day Maurice came home after work and saw a stranger sitting at the kitchen table with his mother. The stranger was a skinny man about his mother's age, and when he looked at Maurice, he smiled.

"Who is this?" Maurice asked his mother.

"Maurice, this is your father."

Maurice was shocked. His father? This skinny old man? Maurice didn't recognize him at all. He hadn't seen his father since he was six years old, but, still, he thought he remembered what he looked like, and he didn't look anything like this man sitting in the kitchen. But then Maurice looked closer. Sure enough, he recognized his father's eyes.

But that only made him angrier.

"What's he doing here?" Maurice asked his mother.

"He wanted to see us again," she replied.

"Get him out of here," Maurice said, and stormed out of the apartment.

After so long Maurice wasn't at all happy to see his father. His father abandoned him when he was just a child, and now— when Maurice was older and could take care of himself—he wanted to be part of his life again? No way. No way, no way, no way. Maurice didn't want to have anything to do with his father. If he never saw him again, that would be just fine.

A few hours later, when Maurice came back home, his father was no longer there. But he lived nearby, which meant that every now and then Maurice would see his father on the street. When he saw him, he would cross the street to avoid him. He didn't even want to give his father the chance to explain why he hadn't cared enough about them to stick around.

One day, when Maurice was walking home, he spotted his father across the street. Then he saw his father fall down. Something was wrong. *Well, that's his problem, not mine,* Maurice told himself. But something inside him made him feel sorry for the old man. He ran across the street and helped his father up.

"What's the matter with you?" Maurice asked him.

"I'm sick, son," he said. "I'm dying."

It was yet another shock for Maurice. His father was skinny

and weak because he had an illness that couldn't be cured. Now Maurice felt bad for him. He was still angry, but he also felt compassion. He sat his father down on the steps of the apartment stoop and sat right next to him.

"Can I ask you something?" Maurice said.

"Yeah, sure."

"Why did you have to be that way?" Maurice asked his father. "Why did you always have to be so mean to Mom, and why did you have to walk out on your family? You were our father. I should have wanted to grow up to be just like you. Why'd you have to be the way you were?"

Junior looked up at Maurice and spoke in a soft voice.

"Because," he said, "it was the only way I knew. No one ever showed me another way. That's the way I thought I had to be."

To Maurice, his father's answer made sense. It was honest. Junior didn't have any role models to show him how to be a better man, a better father. What chance did he have to be anyone but who he was?

"Listen, son, I want to say something else," Junior said. "I am sorry. You don't know how sorry I am. I didn't want to hurt you or your mother or your sisters. I love you all. And I'm sorry I did that to you. I really am."

Maurice didn't say anything. He wasn't sure what to say. *That's okay?* No. It wasn't okay, but he had come to terms with that a long time ago.

"Maybe this was my way of teaching you a lesson," Junior

went on. "And the lesson was—do not be like me. Do not grow up to be like me. Now at least you know what *not* to do."

Maurice struggled for the right words. He felt bad for his father, and he believed his father was truly sorry about the things he'd done. And now he was dying, and he wouldn't have the chance to make things better. All he could do was apologize to his family and hope they accepted his apology.

They sat there for a while, not saying anything. Until, finally, Junior spoke.

"There's one more thing, Maurice," he said. "I know I never did nothing for you in your life, but there's something I want you to do for me."

"What's that?" Maurice asked.

"The one thing I ask," Junior said, "is that when you grow up and have a son of your own, you give him the same name as you and me—Maurice. Can you do that for me, son?"

When he was younger, Maurice loved that he had the same name as his father, because it made him feel connected to something bigger than himself—to a family, and even to their history. But as the years went on, and his father disappeared, Maurice began to dislike his name. He hated how it reminded him of his absent father. And now Junior wanted him to name his own son Maurice too? *No way*, Maurice thought. *Not a chance.*

But, still, he told his father, "Yeah, okay, I'll do it."

"Thank you, son," Junior said.

After that day Maurice continued to see his father on the

street, except now, when he saw him, he would stop and talk to him and ask how he was doing. He wasn't exactly friendly with his father, but he wasn't hostile, either. Maurice figured that stopping to talk to him didn't mean he was forgiving him. It was just a way to be nice to a sick old man.

One day, a neighbor told Maurice his father had died that morning. It was Halloween day. Maurice hurried to the apartment where his father had been staying and found him lying on the floor beside a mattress. Maurice bent down and picked up his father, laying him on the bed. He was startled by how light he was. The toughest guy in Brooklyn, the king of the Tomahawks, was now just skin and bones. Maurice waited until an ambulance arrived. He watched the EMTs take his father away. Then he left the apartment and walked into the street.

19

MAURICE COULD TELL THAT ever since Laura moved out of the city, she worked really hard to keep their Monday night tradition intact. They came up with a plan where every Monday morning, Maurice would find a pay phone and call Laura collect at work to confirm that she was coming in to see him later that day. In Laura's office, her assistant knew it was always okay to accept a call from Maurice. And if, for some reason, they didn't manage to connect on the phone, that meant that they should meet in their usual spot anyway.

Laura tried so hard not to miss a Monday. Here and there, something would come up and she'd tell Maurice that she couldn't make it that week. At one point Laura missed two Mondays in a row. But that was very rare, and the longest Maurice had ever gone without seeing Laura was three weeks. Usually they met at least three out of four Mondays a month. It was clear to Maurice that Laura was trying her best to keep things as consistent as possible between them, while juggling her new relationship with Michael.

For Maurice, seeing Laura on Mondays was as important and meaningful as ever. He could tell that their meetings were just as meaningful to Laura. Just getting the chance to talk and tell each other about their lives was good for both of them. And for Maurice, Laura's continued support gave him the confidence to believe in his own abilities, and in his future.

Another thing had changed. Laura told Maurice that her sister Annette and her family had decided to leave Long Island and move down to Florida. This meant no more trips out to Annette's house. Maurice could tell Laura felt very sad about her sister leaving too.

"I know how much you loved visiting with her and Bruce and the kids," Laura said. "And I did, too. Ever since our mother died, Annette has always been the glue that holds our entire family together. I'm going to miss her."

By then Maurice was getting to know Laura's boyfriend, Michael. He got the chance to meet him a few times, and occasionally the three of them would have dinner, and in those times Michael was always pleasant. He was also kind and generous to Laura, and Maurice was happy to see that. They were clearly in love, and they seemed to make each other very happy. Yet while Michael was friendly enough, Maurice also sensed that he had built a wall around himself, and getting past that wall would be nearly impossible. Or maybe it was that Michael simply didn't want Maurice to be a part of his life with Laura? In any case, Maurice understood that sometimes people build up walls to stay protected.

After all, he had built one around himself, too.

In their own ways, Maurice's mother and his grandmother had tried to teach Maurice the lessons he needed in order to survive in their world. And those lessons were all about being tough, not trusting anyone outside the family, and doing what he needed to do to protect himself from people who wanted to harm him. In a way, those lessons were about turning Maurice into a strong man. Other people might not have seen them that way, but then, those people didn't understand the world in which Maurice and his family lived.

In Maurice's world, the odds were stacked against him. As that one man had told him, the odds were that he'd be dead or in jail by the time he reached eighteen.

And because that was his reality, his mother tried to make Maurice as tough as possible, so that he'd be more prepared to survive it when he got older. The lessons she taught him weren't the kind of lessons he could learn from a textbook—and they weren't the same kind of lessons that Laura was trying to teach him.

But Darcella's lessons were important. They were meant to keep Maurice alive.

Then Laura came into the picture.

When Laura entered Maurice's life, he started learning new and different lessons. With Laura's encouragement, Maurice began to envision a future for himself somewhere *beyond* the world where he grew up. Laura's lessons of love and trust and support—of having the courage to dream big—were very important to Maurice. He understood full well that having crossed paths with Laura on the corner of Fifty-Sixth Street and Broadway was a blessing—a blessing that went far beyond Big Macs and French fries and chocolate milk shakes.

But even so, Maurice wasn't a child anymore.

It was time to put those lessons to use and make his way in the world.

The key to it all was making more money. He needed to be responsible and work hard and he could put his earnings toward having his own apartment and buying his own things. His job as a messenger was fine for now, but Maurice had to start to think bigger than that.

Then, sooner than he expected, an opportunity to make a lot of money came along.

Maurice learned that two older boys he knew from the streets had started their own business selling blue jeans. They would buy trendy blue jeans in New York City, then drive them down to North Carolina, where those jeans weren't yet available in stores. Then they would sell the jeans for more than they paid for them in New York. Since a lot of people wanted the newest and trendiest blue jeans, the sales were brisk and business was good. The boys told Maurice that on some trips, they could each make several hundred dollars.

Maurice liked the sound of that. The boys were older than he was, but, like him, they had grown up on the streets. And now they'd found a way to support themselves just as Maurice wished to do. When they offered Maurice the chance to join them on their next trip to North Carolina, Maurice didn't hesitate. He wanted a piece of the action, so he said yes.

Maurice told Grandma Rose that he was going on the trip. He didn't want her worrying about him if he didn't stop by and visit for a while. She understood why he was leaving, but she still seemed worried for him.

"You be careful, child," Rose said. "Keep your wits about you."

"I will, Grandma," Maurice told her. "I promise."

Maurice decided not to tell Laura about his trip. He didn't want to give her something to worry about. One day he would tell her the truth. But for now he would just put Laura out of his mind.

Maurice went with his two new friends, and used some of the money he'd saved from his messenger job to buy blue jeans to take with him. Then they packed all the jeans into old suitcases and got on a Greyhound bus headed south to North Carolina. On the long drive down, Maurice could only think about one thing. He tried and tried to get the thought out of his head, but he couldn't. It just kept coming back, and it kept making him sad.

All he could think about was the look on Laura's face on Monday morning when Maurice didn't call to get together that night. Then the following Monday he did not call and then the next and the next and the next.

20

THE BUS RIDE TO North Carolina took nearly twelve hours. By the time they arrived in Raleigh, the city's capital, Maurice was tired and hungry. His friends had arranged for them to stay in a trailer owned by a man named Crickett. The trailer was parked along a dead-end street. It was old and falling apart, and inside it was messy and hot. But at least it was a place to stay, and, anyway, Maurice had slept in much worse places.

After a long night of barely sleeping at all—it was just too hot inside the trailer—Maurice and his friends set out with their stash of blue jeans. Selling them, however, turned out to be a lot harder than Maurice had expected. They would set up on a corner somewhere with their suitcases full and do their best to draw people's attention.

In some locations, the owners of nearby stores weren't too happy to see them selling anything on the street, and they would come out of their stores and chase them away. Sometimes, his friends—who were both pretty tall—would be defiant and yell and scream back at the owners. Before Maurice knew it, there would be a full-blown fight on the street.

Maurice had seen how his uncles reacted when fights broke out—they'd always jumped in and tried to prove they were the toughest guys there. They didn't stand around watching or run away—they got right in and fought. And now Maurice, much as he wanted to steer clear of any trouble, found himself right in the middle of the fighting. And every time he did, he remembered what Laura had always told him:

"Maurice, fight with your brain, not with your fists."

Things weren't much better back at Crickett's trailer. There, his friends would get into more fights with Crickett's friends. Someone would say something, and the other person would get angry, and in an instant punches would be thrown. Maurice was always the youngest person there, but that didn't seem to matter to anyone. He was expected to stand up for himself just like everyone else, even if he was the youngest one in the bunch.

Every day there was some new problem. One day his friend began talking to a woman who was the girlfriend of one of Crickett's friends—who wasn't at all happy about it. That started yet another fight. The next day some men who lived near Crickett's trailer came by and told his friends that they had better leave town or else there would be serious trouble. They refused and kicked the men out of the trailer. It got to where Maurice had to look over his shoulder every minute of every day, in case someone else was coming after him. For the first time, he truly understood what that man had told him about never reaching eighteen. In this world, there were a lot of ways for people to get hurt.

And one of those ways was by hanging around the wrong people.

One evening in the trailer, Maurice watched Crickett open his small closet and come out with something wrapped in a towel. He put it down on a table and unwrapped it.

It was a gun.

Maurice had seen guns before. Back in New York City, some people he knew owned and carried guns. That was just part of the reality. But he'd never been this close to a gun, and he'd never stayed in the home of someone who owned a gun. The sight of it made Maurice feel sick.

"I got plenty of guns," Crickett announced. "Plenty for all of us."

The next morning Maurice decided to go to church. He didn't go to church very often, but after all the fighting, and now the gun, Maurice needed the peacefulness of a nearby Pentecostal church. Maurice sat through the morning service, and on his way out, he walked right past the preacher.

"Hold on, son," the preacher said to him. "I need to talk to you."

He pulled Maurice aside and looked him straight in the eyes.

"Son, I don't know what you're doing here in Raleigh, but the Lord is telling me it is time for you to go home," he said.

Maurice was confused. What did the preacher know about anything?

"The Lord says he has work for you to do back home," the preacher went on. "So get yourself back there. If you don't leave now, there will be dire consequences. Your place isn't here, son. Your place is at home."

Maurice left the church without saying a word to the preacher. He couldn't leave Raleigh yet; he still had business to do. Even so, the preacher's words stuck with him.

Your place isn't here. Your place is at home.

In the end, Maurice shrugged off the preacher's warning. Maurice wasn't a child anymore; he didn't need some preacher to protect him. He would stay in North Carolina for as long as it took for him to make the money he needed to make.

That night, in Crickett's trailer, Maurice was getting ready to fall asleep when he heard the loud screech of car tires. He looked out the small trailer window and saw a black car slam to a stop across the street. Then he saw four men jump out of the car and rush right at the trailer.

All four men had guns.

Maurice heard a loud gunshot. A bullet ripped through the side of the trailer and tore into the refrigerator.

"RUN!" Maurice heard Crickett scream.

Maurice bolted out of the trailer and hid behind a parked car. He peeked around it and saw the four men advancing toward him. His friends were next to him, hiding behind another parked car. Then Crickett came out of the trailer, carrying a bag.

Another gunshot rang through the night.

Crickett crouched next to Maurice.

"Here," he told him, "take this."

Crickett reached into the bag and pulled out a gun. He put the gun on the sidewalk right next to Maurice.

"Take it!" Crickett yelled. "Pick it up!"

Maurice looked at the gun on the ground. It was black, and it had a thick handle. It had a rolling chamber that Maurice knew was filled with six bullets. Crickett handed two more guns to Maurice's friends, and kept one for himself. Then he turned back to Maurice.

"Pick up the gun!" he said. "PICK IT UP!"

Another deafening shot rang out. Maurice heard the bullet whiz over his head. He crouched down even tighter to the ground. He'd never felt more afraid in his whole life. And, still, Crickett kept on him.

"You're a man now," he told Maurice. "You're not no child no more. Pick up the gun. Right now."

Another shot rang out, and the bullet shattered the glass window of the car Maurice and Crickett were hiding behind. Bits of glass rained down on his head.

Maurice looked at the gun on the ground. Slowly, he reached out his right hand.

Maurice picked up the gun.

21

Two and a Half Years Later

IT WAS A WARM, breezy day, one of the first really nice days of spring. Everyone's winter jackets were back in the closet, replaced by sweaters, skirts, and even shorts. All along Broadway, people heading to work walked a little less quickly, slowing down to enjoy the sunshine.

Some of those people funneled into a towering office building on Fiftieth Street and Sixth Avenue—across from Radio City Music Hall. It was part of what was known as Rockefeller Center. Those people entered into a wide lobby surrounding a bank of more than thirty elevators, going all the way up to the top floor, the forty-eighth. One of those people was an assistant in her twenties named Rachel. Rachel took the elevator up to the twenty-eighth floor and settled behind her desk in front of a row of offices.

Sometime just after lunch that day, Rachel's telephone rang. She quickly picked it up.

"Hi, is Laura there?" a person said.

"May I say who's calling?" Rachel asked.

Then her eyes grew wide and she nearly dropped the phone.

"Hold on just a second. I'll get her," she quickly said.

She got up from behind her desk, ran toward one of the offices, and knocked on the door.

"Laura," she said to the woman in the office, "I have a phone call for you."

"Who is it?" Laura asked.

"It's Maurice."

Rachel knew who Maurice was. Laura had mentioned him to her quite often. She also knew Maurice had been missing for a long time.

"Did you say 'Maurice'?" Laura asked.

"Yes, Maurice!"

"Oh my goodness!" Laura practically screamed. "Put him through to me!"

On the other end of the phone call, Maurice waited for Laura to pick up. All of a sudden, he heard her scream out his name.

"Maurice!"

"Laura!" Maurice said, his own voice rising. "It's so good to hear your voice again!"

"Maurice, are you okay? Is everything okay?" Laura asked.

Then Maurice got quiet.

"I need to talk to you about something," he finally said. "Can we meet?"

"How about we meet for dinner tonight?" Laura said. "I'll change my plans and we can meet at Michael Jordan's Steak House in Grand Central Station at six p.m. Will that work for you?"

Maurice said that it would, and they agreed to meet for dinner.

"Maurice, I have been so worried about you," Laura said before hanging up. "I have missed you so much."

On the way to the restaurant, Maurice wondered if Laura would be mad at him. On the phone, she didn't seem angry, but how could she not be mad? After all, he'd disappeared without a word. She had every reason to be upset with him. When he got to the steak house, he saw that Laura was already seated at a table, waiting. He walked over to the table, not sure what to expect.

When she saw him, Laura jumped out of her chair and gave Maurice the biggest hug she had ever given him.

"Maurice, I can't believe you're standing here in front of me," Laura said. "I thought about you every day. I wondered where you were or if you were okay. Sometimes I'd be walking and I'd look up and see someone who looked like you, and I'd get so excited. But it was never you."

"I'm sorry I disappeared," Maurice said.

"That's okay," Laura said. "But please tell me why you left. What happened?"

Maurice took a deep breath, and told Laura his story.

Maurice explained to Laura how his goal was to make enough money to support himself and a family of his own. He told her about his friends' business selling jeans, and their trip down to North Carolina. He told her about all the fights they got themselves into. He described the night he heard the screech of tires outside Crickett's trailer.

When four men with guns came out of nowhere and started shooting at him.

"I hid behind a car," Maurice said. "The shots were flying over my head. Then Crickett handed me one of his guns and told me to pick it up."

Laura looked like she was in shock.

"A gun?" she said. "Oh, Maurice."

Maurice told Laura that he reached down and picked up the gun in his hand. He told her how he stared at the gun as bullets kept flying all around him. He told her how he thought about his father, and how tough he was, and what his father would have done in the same situation. And his uncles, and his uncles' friends, and pretty much everyone he knew.

"Then what?" Laura asked.

"Then," Maurice said, "I thought about you."

He explained how, in those terrible moments, with gunshots ringing in his ears and shattered glass spraying everywhere, he thought about everything she'd ever told him. *Don't be late. Punctuality is important. Stop fighting. Do your homework. Stay in school. Make the right choices. Be kind to others. Stay focused. Work hard. Avoid bad people.*

Maurice didn't think about every single thing—there wasn't that much time. But all her words, all her lessons, seemed to roll up into one single powerful thought, which forced its way into Maurice's head as he crouched behind the parked car, afraid for his life.

Be a straight arrow.

Be a straight arrow.

Maurice explained how he put the gun down and never touched it again. After a few more seconds of gunfire, the shooting stopped, and the four men got in their car and drove away. Maurice was still alive. Crickett looked over at him and saw the gun lying on the ground.

"Man, why didn't you shoot the gun?" he yelled at Maurice. "What are you, a baby?"

"This isn't me," Maurice said to Crickett. "I don't belong here. I'm going home."

Then Maurice got up and ran away from the trailer, and not much later he was on a Greyhound bus heading back to New York City.

"You see," Maurice explained to Laura, "all the stuff you taught me, I didn't know if it was ever gonna be useful in my world, 'Cause it's so different from your world. But it turned out that everything you taught me *was* useful. Laura, you saved me."

Laura wiped the tears from her eyes and took Maurice's hand in hers.

"Oh, Maurice, don't you get it?" she said. "You also saved *me!* The truth is, we saved each other."

Maurice shared the rest of his story, telling Laura how he came back to New York City and went back to working as a messenger. How, sadly, his grandma Rose had passed away. How his mother had finally cured her sickness once and for all, and had become more loving and attentive than she had ever been. And how, soon after, his mother got hit with a new illness that made her skinny and weak and frail. How this new illness wasn't something she could hope to recover from.

Maurice explained that his mother was moved to a hospital room. He told Laura he spent every hour he could sitting beside her bed. They talked about this and that, and read from the Bible, and grew closer than they'd been before. One day his mother even asked him about Laura.

"Whatever happened to that woman?" she asked. "The one who was so nice to you?"

Maurice was surprised his mother even remembered who Laura was. They had never talked about her before.

"You mean Laura?" Maurice said. "I haven't seen her in a while."

"Do you know who she was to you, Maurice?" his mother asked.

"No, Momma, who?"

"She was your angel. She was your guardian angel."

Maurice told Laura how he left the hospital believing his mother was slowly getting better. And how, later that night, he got a phone call from his sister LaToya.

"Mom died," she told Maurice.

The words barely made sense. Maurice got up and went back to the hospital.

His mother was still lying in her bed, and she looked the same as when he'd left her. She looked like she was sleeping. Maurice wasn't sure how he should feel at that moment. There were so many emotions running through him—anger, sadness, confusion. Then he noticed his mother's face, and saw that she was smiling. All the pain and sickness and struggle she had endured over the years, it was gone now, all of it. His mother was finally at peace.

"Yes, that's my mother," Maurice told the doctor. "My wonderful mother."

Then Maurice bent over and hugged his mother one last time, kissed her on the forehead, and said his final good-bye.

"I love you, Momma."

Maurice attended his mother's funeral, and right afterward he called Laura at her office. He had remembered her telephone number from years earlier. And now he sat across from her in the restaurant, sharing his story.

"I wanted to prove that I was a man, that I didn't need you to support me," Maurice said, trying to explain why he hadn't called her earlier. "But when my mom died, I realized that I *do* need you. You see, in my whole life, there have only been a handful of people who truly cared about me. And I lost one of them when I lost my grandmother, and I lost another one when I lost my mother. And I just couldn't stand to lose one more, and I knew I had to call you."

Across from him, Laura wiped another tear from her eye.

"Miss Laura," Maurice told her, "you're my mother now."

After a while Maurice turned the conversation to Laura's life.

"Did you and Michael finally have a baby yet?"

The smile on Laura's face went away.

"Not exactly," she said. "Michael already has two sons from his first marriage, and he doesn't want any more children. I tried to persuade him to change his mind, but he never did, and he never will. Maybe I wasn't meant to have my own family."

"Miss Laura, don't say that," Maurice said. "You *do* have a family. *I'm* your family. And you are my family. That will never change."

Laura looked at Maurice and found her smile again.

"How'd you get so much smarter in just two and a half years?" she said.

After they finished dinner, Maurice stayed with Laura while she waited for her train to Westchester in Grand Central Station. As they stood on the track platform, Maurice told Laura something else he'd realized over the past years.

"Miss Laura, I consider my childhood a gift," he said. "As hard as it was, it taught me the right way to raise my own children. I saw what my father did, and I might have grown up thinking that was the only way to be a dad. But then I met you, and you taught me there was another way."

Laura smiled and fought the urge to cry. She looked at Maurice as if she could hardly believe how much he'd grown—

how he was no longer a young boy but a young man.

"Do you know why I told you that you saved me?" she asked.

"No, why?"

"Because all my life, I carried the bad things in my childhood around with me, and they made me sad. But then I met you, Maurice, and you were so brave. You taught me the most valuable lesson about life. You taught me not to feel bad about the things I don't have, and instead to feel blessed by the things I *do* have. You taught me that the true blessings in life are often right there in front of you, maybe even standing on a corner holding out their hand. And that's how you saved me, Maurice."

Now it was Maurice's turn to wipe away a tear.

"What are you going to do now, Maurice?" Laura asked.

Maurice took a deep breath.

"I'm going to get my high school diploma," he said. "And after that I want to become the first person in my family to ever go to college."

"Maurice, that's wonderful," Laura said. "I have no doubt you will."

They said good-bye and made plans to meet again that coming Monday—picking up right where they left off.

And as Maurice walked to the subway that would take him to Brooklyn, he thought about the future. So many times Laura had asked him what he wanted to do with his life, and so many times Maurice had shrugged and said, "I don't know." But now he did know. He was as sure of it as he had ever been of anything before.

That guy was wrong, Maurice thought with a smile. He realized he had made it even beyond eighteen and he was still here and more alive than ever!

My life isn't ending—in fact, it's just beginning.

Postscript

OVER THE YEARS LAURA told lots of people the story of her friendship with Maurice, and they all urged her to write a book about their unlikely encounter with destiny. So in 2007, Laura began writing *An Invisible Thread*. Along with her cowriter, Alex Tresniowski, she made sure Maurice contributed to his side of the story, and she arranged for all three to be partners in the book.

The name of the book comes from an ancient Chinese proverb:

> An invisible thread connects those who are
> destined to meet, regardless of time, place, and
> circumstance. The thread may stretch or tangle.
> But it will never break.

Neither Laura nor Maurice ever imagined how their simple story would ultimately become a #1 *New York Times* bestselling book that continues to resonate with hundreds of thousands of people across the country and around the world. But its central theme—that a simple act of kindness can make an enormous difference, and can even change a person's life—truly connected with readers.

Since the release of *An Invisible Thread* in 2011, Laura has spoken at more than three hundred schools, charity events, organizations, libraries, and local bookstores about the power of a simple act of kindness. She encourages her audiences to explore their own invisible thread connections and to appreciate the love, goodness, and support they have in their lives. She could not be prouder that today schools use *An Invisible Thread* as a teaching guide.

Laura and Maurice's true story took place in the 1980s. But even today there are many, many children like Maurice who aren't sure where their next meal will come from. Across the country, some fourteen million children still go to bed—and to school—hungry. They are children who live in households that are considered "food insecure." Many, like Maurice, go to sleep in the only clothes they own.

Throughout Laura's journey, she has discovered so many amazing organizations that are devoted to helping alleviate many of the problems that children like Maurice and their families endure every day. These organizations, on both the local and national level all across the United States, are focused on assisting underprivileged children and families who need all our support. If you were at all touched by Laura and Maurice's story, please check to see which organizations in your area might be of interest to you. And remember—one small act of kindness can make an enormous difference, and in some cases it can even change a life.

Some Simple Acts of Kindness to Incorporate into Your Day

- Hold the door open for someone.
- Smile at someone you might normally ignore.
- Invite someone to your party or for a play date because you know they want to be your friend.
- Don't exclude someone because they look different.
- Tell a friend how nice they look.
- Send a handwritten thank-you note.
- Help an elderly neighbor by taking out their garbage, helping to wash their car, mowing their lawn, or shoveling their driveway. Or just go over to say hello.
- Invite a classmate to play with you during recess and don't let a classmate eat alone at school.
- Donate your toys and books to children who are less fortunate.
- Thank the people who serve you lunch every day, and let them know how much you enjoyed it.
- Thank the people who keep your school so sparkling clean.
- Make your bed or clean up your room without being told to do it.

- Help someone carry their groceries to their car.
- Ask a friend who is struggling in school if they need help with their homework or a project.
- Say you are sorry after teasing a sibling or a friend.
- Put your phone and iPad down at dinner without being told.
- Be sure to thank the grandparent, aunt, or uncle who might be helping your parents when they need support.
- Make someone smile if you think they are sad.
- Ask to set the table.
- Take your dog for a walk without being told to do it.
- Let someone go ahead of you in line.
- Bake a dessert for someone who is sick.
- Write a thank-you note to your teacher.
- Set up a lemonade stand and donate the money to a charity of your choice.
- Tell your teacher or parents immediately if you think someone in your class or neighborhood is being bullied and always remember it's never okay to be a bully or to watch someone being bullied.
- And finally, always remember to be kind. Kindness is contagious and the more you incorporate small acts of kindness in your daily life, the more you will want to do it over and over again.

left: Laura's mother, Marie, and her father, Nunzie, on their wedding day in February 1949 on Long Island.

right: Laura's first communion, in 1958. Laura is in a special dress with (from left) her baby sister, Nancy (sitting on her father's knee); her brother Frank; and her sister Annette.

The Carino kids in the mid-1960s: (from left) Frank, Laura, Annette, Nancy, and Steven.

Here Laura is in pigtails hanging out with her high school friends Darcy (center) and Sue. The Mustang belonged to Darcy's parents.

below: An old photo of Maurice's extended family. That's his mother, Darcella (holding Maurice's sister, center), and his grandmother Rose (far right).

above: Laura and her friend Barbara graduating from Walt Whitman High School in 1970.

right: Laura in her West 56th Street studio apartment at the Symphony. It was only one room, but it was her sanctuary.

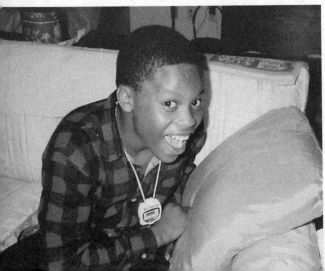

That's Maurice on one of his visits to Laura's apartment in 1986. He's wearing the watch Laura bought to help him get to school on time.

left: Laura took Maurice to ride the carousel in Central Park in 1986. Laura could always tell Maurice was having fun by his smile.

below: Maurice in Central Park.

above: Maurice and Laura on the outdoor running track on the tenth floor of her Manhattan apartment building in 1986.

right: Maurice in Laura's apartment in 1986. He's wearing some sweats Laura gave him while they did his laundry.

Maurice loved visiting Annette's house in Greenlawn, New York. Maurice couldn't believe how big the front lawn was.

Annette and her husband, Bruce, at home with their wonderful kids, (from left) Derek, Brooke, and Colette.

Maurice fit right in. Here they all are hanging out in Laura's apartment on Thanksgiving Day, 1986.

We all watched the Macy's Thanksgiving Day parade from the outdoor running track overlooking Broadway. The floats seemed close enough to touch!

Maurice opening Laura's first Christmas present to him—a remote-control race car—on Christmas Eve, 1986. Her sister Nancy is giving him a hand.

The Carino kids, all grown up, at Annette's house on Christmas Day, 1986: (from left) Frank, Nancy, Laura, Annette, and Steven.

Maurice and Derek in 1989. Laura bought Maurice a new Ross chrome ten-speed bike. Boy, was he surprised.

below: Laura and her future husband, Michael, at the Il San Pietro Hotel in Positano, Italy, in 1989.

above: Laura's brother Frank (April 19, 1954–June 20, 1995) in his navy uniform in 1975. He served for just under three years.

right: Laura's girls! These were her poodles, Lucy (on the left) and Coco, in her condo in East Moriches, New York. She will always love and miss them.

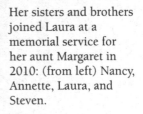

Her sisters and brothers joined Laura at a memorial service for her aunt Margaret in 2010: (from left) Nancy, Annette, Laura, and Steven.

Maurice and his family at the funeral for his mother, Darcella, in 2000: (from left, back row) Maurice (holding Jahleel), Ikeem, and Maurice's wife, Michelle; (front row) Jalique, Princess, and Maurice Jr.

Maurice and Michelle helped Laura celebrate her fiftieth birthday at the Westchester Country Club in October 2001.

Maurice gave an emotional toast at Laura's birthday celebration in 2001. "You saved my life," Maurice told her. "The Lord sent me an angel. And my angel was Laurie."

Maurice and his family today: (back row) Ikeem; (center row, from left) Jalique, Laura, Maurice Jr., Princess, Maurice, and Michelle; (front row) Jahleel, Jahmed, and Precious.

Maurice's dream came true! This is his family gathered around their really big dining room table in downtown Manhattan: (from left) Michelle, Princess, Precious, Jahmed, and Jahleel.

November 2011, at *An Invisible Thread* book launch party:

Laura with her family.

Laura and Maurice with his family.

Laura, Maurice, and cowriter Alex Tresniowski.

Laura Schroff is an international and #1 *New York Times* best-selling author and keynote speaker. Since the launch of her books, *An Invisible Thread; An Invisible Thread Christmas Story*; and *Angels on Earth: Inspiring Real-Life Stories of Fate, Friendship, and the Power of Kindness*, Laura has become a passionate and compelling voice on the power of acts of kindness and human connections. Laura is a former advertising executive who worked with major media companies, including Time Inc. and Condé Nast, and was part of the *USA Today* advertising launch team and worked at *Ms.* magazine. Born and raised on Long Island, New York, Laura lives in Westchester with her poodle, Emma.

Alex Tresniowski is a former human-interest writer at *People* and the bestselling author of several books, most notably *The Vendetta*, which was purchased by Universal Studios and used as a basis for the movie *Public Enemies*. His other titles include *An Invisible Thread*, *Waking Up in Heaven*, and *The Light Between Us*.